MW00826403

Thinking as Though God Exists

Newman on Evangelizing the "Nones"

THINKING
as though
GOD EXISTS

Newman on
Evangelizing the "Nones"

Ryan N.S. Topping

First published in the USA
by Angelico Press 2023

For information, address:
Angelico Press
169 Monitor St.
Brooklyn, NY 11222
www.angelicopress.com

978-1-62138-905-7 (pbk)
978-1-62138-906-4 (cloth)
978-1-62138-907-1 (ebook)

CONTENTS

Abbreviations

Works by Cardinal Newman

Unless otherwise noted, references are to the uniform edition published by Longmans, Green & Co. between 1868 and 1881, in most cases available online by the kind offices of the *National Institute for Newman Studies*. When two dates are given below, the first indicates the original date of publication.

Apo	*Apologia Pro Vita Sua* (1864/1873)
BS	"Biglietto Speech" (1879) in *Addresses to Cardinal Newman with His Replies*, ed. W.P. Neville (Longmans, Green & Co., 1905)
Cal	*Callista: A Tale of the Third Century* (1855)
DMC	*Discourses to Mixed Congregations* (1849)
ECH	*Essays Critical and Historical*, 2 vols. (1871–85)
GA	*An Essay in Aid of a Grammar of Assent* (1870)
Idea	*Idea of a University* (1852), ed. Martin J. Svaglic (South Bend, IN: University of Notre Dame Press, 1982)
Letter	*A Portrait in Letters*, ed. Roderick Strange (Oxford: Oxford University Press, 2015)
LD	*Letters and Diaries of John Henry Newman*, ed. Charles Stephen Dessain, et al. (Oxford: Clarendon Press, 1978–2008)
LDN	*Letter to the Duke of Norfolk* in *Certain Difficulties Felt by Anglicans in Catholic Teaching*, vol 2 (1875)
LG	*Loss and Gain* (1848)
LPC	*Lectures on the Present Position of Catholics in England* (1851)

MD	*Meditations and Devotions of the Late Cardinal Newman*, ed. William P. Neville (London: Longmans, 1893)
OS	*Sermons Preached on Various Occasions* (1857)
PPS	*Parochial and Plain Sermons* (1868)
Serm	*Sermons Preached on Various Occasions*, 1824–1843, 5 vols.
US	*University Sermons, Preached Before the University of Oxford* (1826–43/1872)
VV	*Verses on Various Occasions* (1867)

Other Works

AEB	Benedict XVI, "Address at the Vigil on the Eve of the Beatification of Newman" (London, Sept. 18, 2010)
CCC	The Catechism of the Catholic Church
DRV	The Holy Bible, Douay-Rheims Version (London: Baronius Press, 2015)
RM	John Paul II, *Redemptoris Missio*, On the Permanent Validity of the Church's Missionary Mandate (1990)
ST	St. Thomas Aquinas, *Summa Theologiae*
TMA	John Paul II, *Tertio Millennio Adveniente* (1994)

Preface

Since joining the Catholic Church I have always wanted to get to know John Henry Newman better. It was reading his *Apologia* just prior to our conversion, some fifteen years ago, that laid the last stone my wife and I needed to step across the uncertain waters of the Tiber onto the solid Roman shore. In the months leading up to our reception I also spent time in retreat at Newman's quasi-monastic farm in Littlemore, a few miles outside of Oxford; there, under the shadow of the master, I collected as best as I could my own scattered thoughts about the graces I'd received as a Protestant, about the legacy of the Church Fathers, about the ministry of "Peter," and about whether God was not, indeed, asking of us the same act of submission that He required of the great Cardinal over a century before. He did ask, and by grace, we were received. Life and work moved along, and Newman was confined largely to our memory, until recently.

In 2010 Pope Benedict XVI's widely televised Apostolic Journey to the United Kingdom returned the world's attention once more to the saintly scholar. The Holy Father's beatification of Newman opened the path to canonization, which came, after a second confirmed miracle, sooner than anyone guessed. And in 2019 the Church welcomed into its midst Newman the Saint. The saint is a rare type. The saint is not the one who has lost his freedom; the saint is the one who has lost everything except his freedom. These are men and women drawn from all classes and every circumstance of life, but with this difference: they are confined to none of these. Just as every age breeds its own vices, so also at no time is the Church bereft of heroes. For that is what defines a saint. They are Christian success stories. Their journey turned out well. They made it home. Anyone who has gained familiarity with this type knows well that these "successes" are not without their own failures, temptations, sufferings, and trials; the difference between them and most of us lies chiefly in their fidelity.

Newman's own life and witness show how the Church herself, like each of her members, must live and grow while remaining constant and true to the Faith once delivered. Ours is an age of volubility, tempted as we are by the lure of constant revolutions. Friendship, family, faith, all must dissolve, we are told in a thousand ways, before the undiluted acid of self-interest, or the market. These days, the most basic facts of nature, like the definitions of sex, must bow before the false altar of a feckless freedom. Catholic or not, we are all to one degree or another casualties of the modern project's mad pursuit of the "autonomous self," the philosophy of life that Newman typically described under the banner of "liberalism." Whatever additional characteristics we might wish to ascribe to today's postmodern or post-Christian culture, the ideal of an unbounded freedom that we must counter is the same foe that Newman met. Too many of us, both inside and outside the Church, without tradition, without faith, without fealty, now find ourselves rootless and reeling upon a sea without sight of the shore. In his youth, Newman sailed on similar waters, arriving at his true port only after a tempestuous voyage. But he did arrive. And he reflected long on what was required for a safe return. He serves therefore as an excellent guide for contemporary pilgrims who wish to live in the light of both reason and revelation, that is to say, those who wish to think and act *as though God exists*.

I offer this book not as another introduction to Newman's life, to his Victorian context, or even to his theology in general.[1] Instead, the following reflections take up those parts of Newman's legacy that appear helpful to understanding one of our most urgent tasks: evangelizing our post-Christian culture. The reevangelization of the West requires many things: the rebuilding of the family, the renewal

1. Solid biographies and introductions already serve such purposes. As a start, one may look to Ian Ker's *Newman: A Biography* (Oxford: Oxford University Press, 2009), Sheridan Gilley's *Newman and His Age* (Westminster, MD: Christian Classics, 1990), and Keith Beaumont's *John Henry Newman: Theologian and Spiritual Guide for Our Times* (San Francisco: Ignatius Press, 2010).

of priestly and religious life, the recovery of our artistic traditions, a new outpouring of the gifts of the Holy Spirit, and more. But none of these endeavors can flourish apart from ongoing reflection about the relation between faith and culture. In this book I have in mind two sorts of readers: those who appreciate Newman and those who care about apologetics, broadly understood. For both I aim to show how the method and the substance of Newman's thought can today be credibly applied by ordinary Christians with an interest in the extraordinary project of the New Evangelization.

Each chapter takes up a domain of contemporary culture in need of renewal. My general approach is to describe some threat to the life of faith and then to show where Newman's thought can help us overcome it. Newman has much to contribute to the Church of the twenty-first century. We have for too long ordered our institutions and our personal lives as though we were practical atheists. Even when believers do not wish to think in a godless fashion, we tend to separate the life of faith from our secular, daily pursuits. Another way to put the problem is this. The conditions of our post-Christian culture reinforce a habitual separation of public life from private, of reason from faith. Throughout this book I illustrate Newman's marvelous power to correlate and integrate these now separated realms, to manifest knowledge not only of individual objects, but to achieve a "connected view" of "their mutual and true relations," as he names this effort of intellectual enlargement in Discourse 6 of his *Idea of a University.* My argument is that if the New Evangelization is to succeed, we need also daringly to manifest Newman's same *integrative habit of mind.*[2] This book offers a proof of concept for that thesis.

Individual chapters attempt to make good on this claim within specific domains—among them, ethics, politics, catechesis, preaching, liturgical arts, and education. It is my hope that by observing Newman's manner of approaching problems that confronted his contemporaries, we might think and act with greater wisdom

2. See further Frederick D. Aquino's *An Integrative Habit of Mind: John Henry Newman on the Path to Wisdom* (DeKalb, IL: Northern Illinois University Press, 2012).

toward the problems that address ours. The discussion unfolds in the following order. The opening chapter defines the task of the New Evangelization and establishes why, given our present cultural and ecclesial situation, Newman is integral to this project. Subsequent chapters consider how one trying to think with an *integrated habit of mind* might respond to the damage of the priestly abuse crisis, to the rise of the "nones" as a prominent demographic, to the question of how art and liturgy can order our affections, to the problems of social life raised by public atheism, to three modern myths that ground the case for secularism, to the varying approaches to contemporary apologetics, to the true and false accounts of "conscience" now in circulation, and, finally, to our need for a renewal of the classical liberal arts tradition in education. In each domain, Newman's rich theology offers, so I suggest, powerful resources for implanting or renewing faith and along with it a vibrant Catholic culture.

In the completion of this study I have many people to thank. I begin with my colleagues at Newman Theological College who have allowed me to continue to write and teach alongside my administrative duties. Word of Newman's canonization prompted a desire among us to propose a course on our College's namesake, a public lecture series, a faculty Reading Group on *The Idea of the University*, as well as a national conference "Newman and His Legacy" (commuted due to the pandemic), all of which we hosted in the Archdiocese of Edmonton, Canada, over the 2019–2020 academic year. It was with these events in view that I began the happy work of reading, discussing Newman with others, and writing.

My thanks to the Sisters of *Der Werke* whose hospitality at Littlemore years ago provided my wife and me with an intimate introduction to this English saint. I thank the Oxford Oratorians who so marvelously embody Newman's own mission in their ministry. This community instilled for our family an ideal of parish life that has nourished us over many years. Professor Reinhard Hütter graciously allowed me to view his forthcoming manuscript, now published as *John Henry Newman on Truth and Its Counterfeits: A Guide for Our Times* (Catholic University of America, 2020); I read and benefitted from his work at a late stage in my writing. Mr. Ian

Mahood, Dr. Jason West, and Dr. Bud Marr provided helpful feedback on early drafts of the manuscript. I am grateful for the generous endorsements offered by Brian Holdsworth, Fr. Aidan Nichols, O.P., George Weigel, and Cardinal Thomas Collins. Like many others who dare to write about Newman, I too register a debt of gratitude to the late Fr. Ian Ker whose scholarship at various points has encouraged my own thinking, especially his title *Newman on Vatican II* (Oxford University Press, 2014). Many thanks to John Riess and his staff at Angelico for their good works in Catholic publishing and for their interest in bringing forward this project. Finally, alongside my gratitude to my wife, Anna, I lovingly dedicate this book to our children, whose task it will be to carry forward the work of the New Evangelization: Peter, Joseph, Thomas, Francis, Dominic, Gregory, John Paul, Catherine, Ambrose, and Philip.

1

Newman's New Evangelization

"God has created me to do Him some definite service"[1]

I

The New Evangelization is another name for the reevangelization of post-Christian culture. In the West, banks still close for Christmas and Easter, families reunite for Thanksgiving dinners, politicians invoke God's blessing during times of War, and the recent world pandemic inspired Christlike sacrifices among many. In these and countless other ways, we in the West still inhabit Christian cultures. In other ways, however, Western liberal democracies have become deeply, aggressively, incontrovertibly, and menacingly "post"-Christian. Christianity is older than the "West." Over the Church's long history it has in every regime successfully sought and won converts to its message of salvation. Today, nevertheless, the Church casts its net over a different sort of water. When St. Paul stood before the Athenians, when Patrick landed in Ireland, when Xavier preached in Japan, and Brébeuf on the shores of the St. Lawrence, they could presume in their hearers some notion of divinity that had only to be purified.

Not so today. For many of our contemporaries, the supernatural is either unfamiliar or the object of intense hostility. After centuries of secularization, modern people now find themselves enclosed within an immanent horizon, what Pope John Paul II termed "the

1. *MD* 3.1.2.

eclipse of the sense of God and of man" or what the Canadian philosopher Charles Taylor has called a "self-sufficient humanism."[2] Secularism, as I shall evoke the term, refers to the organization of society *as though God does not exist.* Central to the task of the New Evangelization is to learn again how to think as if he does, as he does truly. Where secularism has triumphed, men and women hold to a vision of the good life that rejects as alien the very idea of the search for fulfillment beyond the material, for ultimate purposes, and consequently, for those questions to which religion has traditionally supplied the answers. And when answers are sought, for such starved souls, it is now often in dark gods that they find their answers.

Given present conditions, the challenge for the Church is not merely to present post-Christian people with the doctrines and precepts of religion; our object is now to arouse in them some feeling for its need, or perhaps to redirect those feelings away from pseudoreligious movements and counterfeits. Our Lord promised that the harvest is always plentiful, but it is also true that each laborer has his own work; ours seems to be that of preparing again the soil. As I hope will become clear through these pages, like St. Augustine in the fourth century, and like St. Thomas during the high Middle Ages, Newman's thought is wonderfully suited to equip the Church of the twenty-first century for precisely this work of evangelization. Indeed, in large measure Newman may be credited with launching what only later came to be called the West's "new" evangelization.

More often it has been observed that the Second Vatican Council (1962–1965) was "Newman's Council." This was a sentiment first echoed by the Pope who led the great gathering. Speaking of Newman ten years after the Council, Paul VI wrote that many of the complicated questions which Newman "treated with wisdom," were themselves debated by "the Fathers of the Second Vatican Council."[3]

2. John Paul II, *Evangelium Vitae, On the Gospel of Life* (1995), 21; Charles Taylor, *A Secular Age* (Cambridge, MA: Belknap Press, 2007), 18.

3. Paul VI, "Address to Newman Scholars" (April 7, 1975), available at the online Newman Reader at Newmanreader.org.

Although Newman is not cited directly in the documents, for those who know where to look, his shadow looms over some key passages. His emphasis on the recovery of the early Church fathers, on the dignity of the laity, on the defense of conscience, and on the theory of doctrinal development, all left indelible marks upon the finished texts.[4]

A generation later, John Paul II promulgated the *Catechism of the Catholic Church*, the chief doctrinal legacy of Vatican II. For pastors, teachers, evangelists, families, and all engaged in the work of evangelization, the *Catechism* serves as the most accessible and comprehensive guide to Christian belief. As a rough illustration of the way Newman has entered magisterial thinking, it is instructive to see the varied appeals which the *Catechism* makes to his work. Newman is quoted more frequently than St. Athanasius, St. Anselm, St. Bonaventure, or St. Ignatius of Loyola, to name a few luminaries. Among theologians writing after 1600, that is, after the reforms of the Council of Trent, only St. Thérèse of Lisieux receives more attention (by one citation). Of those passages in the *Catechism* where Newman is cited, the first explores the psychological nearness of faith to doubt, another on true versus false senses of conscience, yet another on the distinction between simple pleasures and Christian happiness, and the last on the duty to harmonize our feelings with our religious obligations; one other passage, where Newman is cited but not named, concerns how it is that we come to prove and hold with conviction that God exists.[5] This range of topics gives some sense of the breadth and relevance of Newman's interests. His ability to speak beautifully to each of them manifests

4. Though of course not everything in the Council would have been familiar or even would likely have been met with enthusiasm by Newman. See Avery Dulles's measured and detailed list of comparisons and contrasts between themes treated by Newman and at Vatican II in his *Newman* (New York: Continuum, 2002), chapter 10.

5. For the citations see CCC paras 157, 1723, 1778, 2144 and, where Newman is quoted without attribution, 35. (On this last attribution, Newman's discussions of converging and convincing probabilities can be found, for instance, at *Apo* iv, 2 and *GA* part 2, ch. 9, sec. 2.3, and part 2, ch. 10, sec. 2.)

also what is perhaps Newman's most extraordinary gift: his power to integrate. Throughout Newman's writings we find him taking the insights of faith and reason together and then applying them to the task of witnessing to a culture rapidly losing its grip on religion. Indeed, one of the Council's Canadian fathers—who would return from Rome to found a college in Newman's name—reflected that the reason why we need Newman in our time is because the problems he worked on are largely our problems.[6] I believe this judgement is correct. This study aims to illuminate the truth of this claim with respect to evangelization.

II

Still, why Newman now? What can a late Victorian bachelor teach us about postmodern North America? While it is true that Newman lived prior to "cancel culture," prior to the internet, prior to the sexual revolution, prior to both World Wars, the dynamics that gave rise to secularism were already at work one hundred and fifty years ago. Newman observed well. Steeped in the past he saw far into the future. To say this in other words, another reason why Newman's thought continues to prove fecund is that, while he was a master of the Church's intellectual heritage, he grasped what her children were about to inherit. Newman was one of the first great theorists of late modernity. Even during the high mark of Europe's cultural ascendancy, he recognized that the West was soon to turn against itself. He saw that with the rejection of reason would come an attack on faith, especially the faith of Catholics. As he predicted to a group of seminarians in a lecture near the end of his life, the Church was soon to face trials which "would appall and make dizzy even such courageous hearts as St. Athanasius." He foresaw how Catholics in

6. Archbishop Anthony Jordan, O.M.I., armed with this conviction, came back from the Council to found Newman Theological College in Edmonton, Alberta. See his reflection, "Newman Theological College and Cardinal J.H. Newman," paper given at Newman Theological College, March 20, 1979 at www.newman.edu/History.

the future will be thought of as "enemies" of our "civil liberty"; he stated baldly that the persecutions to come would inflict such suffering as has not been seen "since the age of Constantine."[7] Newman expressed more clearly than any others in the nineteenth century, perhaps except for the atheist Friedrich Nietzsche and the pope Leo XIII, the magnitude of the coming tsunami that was to wreak havoc upon Western civilization. As Newman grasped, it is the force of secularism's combined disruptions to our anthropology, philosophy, politics, education, and family life that have together rendered our culture "post"-Christian.

In recent decades Newman's vision for the need for a new evangelization has slowly come into focus for the wider Church. Even though the last Council addressed a range of topics, surprisingly, it hardly mentioned evangelization. The question of how or even why the Church might need to foster a distinctively Christian (counter) culture in the midst of secular modernity seemed largely absent from the mind of the fathers.[8] Arguably, during the mid-twentieth century, it is the nature of the Church itself that received the most sustained attention among leading theologians.[9] During the last decades of the twentieth century, however, Catholicism's strategic shift in emphasis increasingly came to reflect the West's altered cultural situation. Ten years after Vatican II, Paul VI would, in his encyclical *Evangelii Nuntiandi*, become the first pope to redirect the Church's gaze away from questions of its own internal constitution. The pontiff that led the Council and that issued *Humanae Vitae* against artificial contraception instead turned the Church's energy toward a new outward advance.

Then came the quarter-century pontificate of St. John Paul II. He

7. See Newman's Sermon "The Infidelity of the Future" (October 2, 1873), in *Faith and Prejudice*, ed. by the Birmingham Oratory (New York: Sheed and Ward, 1956), included in our appendix.

8. A theme well developed in Tracey Rowland's *Culture and the Thomist Tradition After Vatican Two* (New York: Routledge, 2003).

9. This at least was the view of Pope Paul VI who called the Church the "principal object" of the Council in his *Ecclesiam Suam*, 33; and see Ian Ker, *Newman on Vatican II* (Oxford: Oxford University Press, 2014), 81.

made the "new" evangelization of secularized post-Christians—not the conversion of pagans or Protestants—the object of his mission. Early in his pontificate he described what was new about this call. The Church, the pope explained, is always oriented towards mission. The call to make disciples is not new. What has shifted is the circumstance of culture in which that call has to be made. The Church of our time operates, he proposed, in three situations. In the first, the Church preaches *ad gentes*, to the unbaptized nations which lack the power to "incarnate the faith" in their own time and place. This was Africa in the nineteenth century. In the second, the Church continues her pastoral and missionary efforts among peoples "already fervent in their faith." This was Ireland in the twentieth century. The third "intermediate situation" is uniquely our own. The need for a new or re-evangelization has now become apparent among nations and peoples often of "ancient Christian roots" that have in recent times "lost a living sense of the faith."[10] In such places, many Catholics are marked by "fatigue, disenchantment, compromise, lack of interest" and above all, "lack of joy and hope."[11] This is Europe and North America in the twenty-first century. Thus the Church, we might say, must proclaim her message *ad gentes*, *ad fideles*, and now *ad errantes*—to the lost, to the faithful, and to the wandering. Indeed, by the end of his pontificate, John Paul II had named the "new evangelization" as the hermeneutical key to understanding the Church's present task. In the Apostolic Letter he wrote on the eve of the third Christian millennium the Holy Father even proposed that in retrospect every general and regional synod "begun after the Second Vatican Council" should be understood as aiming to advance nothing other than the "new" evangelization.[12]

This direction was strengthened under Benedict XVI as was the link between Newman and the task set before us. Benedict XVI, arguably the pope intellectually closest to Newman, himself declared that the cardinal has "long been an important influence in

10. John Paul II, RM, 33.
11. Ibid., 36.
12. John Paul II, TMA, 21.

my own life and thought."[13] Similar to the way that Newman sought to counter "Liberalism," Benedict aimed his efforts against the "dictatorship of relativism."[14] This philosopher-pope tailored his own formidable addresses increasingly at secular audiences, or at least at providing for Christians a model of engagement with those who no longer share Christianity's fundamental vision.

Benedict's analysis of modernity's root causes shares striking similarities to Newman's. Like the English saint, this German pope has described well the organic link between modern man's assertion that he is "the sole architect of his nature and destiny" and the "interior desert" that results from this rootlessness.[15] For these two intellectual giants of modern Catholicism, half-measures have little appeal. For the pope and the cardinal, in the face of the rejection of both revelation and the natural law, the new evangelization requires nothing less than the relaunch of a renovated Christian philosophy of life. It is only by recovering the Church's own intellectual, devotional, and artistic traditions—along the model of Newman's recovery of the early Church Fathers—that we will be capable of transforming the thought and the patterns of our technologically progressing yet spiritually drifting post-Christian culture. Alongside Scripture, the liturgy, the fathers, and St. Thomas, the Church of the New Evangelization will no doubt now also draw ever more deeply upon the legacy of St. John Henry Newman. His example of drawing together faith and reason provides hope that we might do the same. To the question: Why Newman now? I reply: because he models *an integrated habit of mind.*

13. Benedict XVI, AEB; see also Tracey Rowland's *Ratzinger's Faith: The Theology of Pope Benedict XVI* (Oxford: Oxford University Press, 2010), especially 2–9, 45, 81–82, and David G. Bonagura's essay, "Newman and Ratzinger" in *The Catholic Thing* (October 5, 2019), www.thecatholicthing.org/2019/10/05/newman-and-ratzinger.

14. Benedict XVI first used the phrase "dictatorship of relativism" in his April 18, 2005 address to the College of Cardinals where he warned: "We are building a dictatorship of relativism that does not recognize anything as definitive and whose ultimate goal consists solely of one's own ego and desires."

15. Benedict XVI, AEB.

This grand project will demand sustained efforts for at least the next fifty years. Benedict XVI seemed to recognize the interconnectedness between the saintly scholar and the reconversion of the West. In 2010, the pope gave both Newman and the New Evangelization more formal recognition within the structure of the Church. In that year, the Holy Father beatified the cardinal and established a Pontifical Council charged with perpetuating the renewal of Christendom, however its next iteration is to look. Following from Benedict's papacy, we note that Francis's own first major document, *Evangelii Gaudium*, also took up evangelization. Making his own the words of John Paul II, he reasserts that "today missionary activity still represents the greatest challenge for the Church."[16] Given the accelerating secularism of the twenty-first century, the need for brave souls to strike out into the currents of secular culture is not likely to diminish. Like all who dare to enter upon the high seas of adventure, we do well to learn from those who have struggled before us and prevailed.

III

John Henry Newman (1801–1890) lived during a century of enormous political, economic, cultural, and religious upheaval. During his life, Catholics still could not hold public office nor attend universities in Britain. In Victorian England, British Protestants widely regarded Catholics as socially backward and educationally inferior, that is, until Newman's conversion. As an Oxford Don, parish priest, and a cultural commentator, by his 40s Newman found himself as the leading public figure in a bid to return the Anglican Communion to a more vibrant and liturgically robust expression of faith. Prophet that he was, he feared that the Reformation had too closely

16. Francis, *Evangelii Gaudium*, 15; for background, see Walter F. Kedjierski, "Papal Contributions to the Development of the Church's Missionary Spirit: From *Ad Gentes* to *Evangelii Gaudium*" in *Logos: A Journal of Catholic Thought and Culture* 21:1 (Winter 2020): 94–110. Though Pope Francis in 2022–2023—on the fiftieth anniversary of the opening of Vatican II—chose to launch a Synod not on evangelization but on "Synodality."

allied itself with subjectivism in religion, and paved the way to agnosticism in politics. Newman was ever a seeker of truth about first principles. His own deep study in religion and philosophy, and particularly of the early Greek Fathers, gradually drew him closer to Catholicism. In 1845, after a long and arduous search, and at great cost to his reputation and career, Newman forsook his eminent position as a man of letters within English society to join the Church of Rome.

For his remaining years Newman devoted his enormous energy to advancing Catholic causes. His scholarly output is staggering. During his life he published some thirty-seven volumes, including a celebrated book of poetry (Edward Elgar composed an oratorio to the text of Newman's poem *The Dream of Gerontius*), two novels, numerous historical and theological works, in addition to about 20,000 letters. Whether it was establishing the Oratorian religious community in England, a school for boys in Birmingham, or the Catholic University of Ireland, Newman was indefatigable in his service for others. Many sought his advice as a guide and friend. He never failed to encourage others, or himself, to heed God's particular call to greatness. As he once reflected:

> God has created me to do Him some definite service. He has committed some work to me which He has not committed to another. I have my mission—I may never know it in this life, but I shall be told it in the next. I am like a link in a chain, a bond of connection between persons. He has not created me for naught. I shall do good, I shall do his work.[17]

Newman's service bore fruit. His generous fidelity and his massive intellectual labor lifted Catholicism in the English-speaking world out of its relative obscurity into a new radiance. The effect of Newman's conversion was immediate. The first wave of converts largely came from among those Anglicans seeking a deeper union with the historic faith, and included such literary luminaries as Oscar Wilde, a deathbed convert, and Gerard Manley Hopkins, perhaps the finest poet of his age—whom Newman received personally in 1866. The

17. *MD* 3.1.2.

second wave of converts was dominated by the likes of Robert Hugh Benson, Ronald Knox and the Catholic apologist and wit G.K. Chesterton, who himself entered the fold in 1922. During the mid-twentieth century, the third wave of converts and others influenced by Newman include the Harvard historian Christopher Dawson, the novelist Evelyn Waugh, as well as the community of imaginative writers known as the Inklings. And the circle continues to widen.

In addition to Newman's impressive contributions to the Church during the last Council, a brief survey of Newman's major works gives some sense of the close connection between his questions and our own. As a poet, Newman added some of the most beloved hymnody to the Church's repertoire in his *Lyra Apostolica* (1836); as a theologian, Newman wrestled with the way that truth can remain constant amidst the expansion and amplification of ideas over time in his *Essay on the Development of Christian Doctrine* (1845); as an educator, he defended the liberal arts as the only humane foundation for learning in his *The Idea of a University* (1852); as a novelist, he elegantly described the movements of a soul toward grace in his *Callista: A Tale of the Third Century* (1855); as an apologist, his spiritual autobiography *Apologia pro Vita Sua* (1864) stands as a compelling testimony to faith against the trials of doubt; as a philosopher, Newman produced a stunningly contemporary analysis of the psychology of belief in his *An Essay in Aid of the Grammar of Assent* (1870); as a debater, he launched his open letter to an English Prime Minister in defense of Catholics' right to participate actively in politics in his *Letter to the Duke of Norfolk* (1875); and so on. In each of these works we see on display how faith and reason and Christian culture integrate into a beautiful whole.

The saint is indeed a rare type, few rarer than Newman. In Newman we find perhaps the greatest of modern saints who faithfully combined sanctity and scholarship, an appealing witness to a profound wisdom of things human and divine. I close these preliminary remarks with the salutary words that Benedict XVI offered on Newman's contribution to our present task:

> The drama of Newman's life invites us to examine our lives, to see them against the vast horizon of God's plan, and to grow in com-

> munion with the Church of every time and place: the Church of the apostles, the Church of the martyrs, the Church of the saints, the Church which Newman loved and to whose mission he devoted his entire life.... Newman's life also teaches us that passion for the truth, intellectual honesty and genuine conversion are costly. The truth that sets us free cannot be kept to ourselves; it calls for testimony, it begs to be heard, and in the end its convincing power comes from itself and not from the human eloquence or arguments in which it may be couched.[18]

An integrated habit of mind: reuniting faith with reason, head with heart, sanctity with suffering, tradition with the Church's ongoing mission: these are themes running throughout Newman's work and these pages, and these are the skills we need to recover if we too are to think again of our faith and our culture as though God exists.

18. Benedict XVI, AEB.

2

A Bride with Blemishes

"Rome must change first of all in her spirit"[1]

I

No one today could say that it is easy being Catholic. This discomfort is caused not only by persecution. Priestly sexual scandals, corruption among some bishops, and the lack of moral clarity at the highest levels of the Church have aggravated a growing sense of insecurity among the faithful. Each age nurtures its own vices. Ours are not chiefly failures of pride or lust. The blemishes that most disfigure the Bride of Christ today are the fruit of another sort of failure, of weak love, of what the Church fathers called *acedia*. Weak love arises in souls that lack conviction, souls that are paralyzed by the gnawing claws of doubt. In North America Mass attendance has plummeted; in some places, Catholic teens fornicate as much as their irreligious classmates; church weddings, like new vocations, have become in some regions ceremonies of novelty. By virtually any metric, the Church militant in North America is suffering.[2]

In St. Paul's Epistle to the Romans he calls the Church the "Bride

1. *LD* viii, 42, to J. R. Bloxam.

2. For background studies, see Sherry Weddell, *Forming Intentional Disciples* (Huntington, IN: Our Sunday Visitor, 2012), Ryan Topping, *Rebuilding Catholic Culture* (Manchester, NH: Sophia Institute Press, 2012), Christian Smith with Melina Denton, *Soul Searching: The Religious and Spiritual Lives of American Teenagers* (New York: Oxford University Press, 2005), and William V. D'Antonio, et al., *American Catholics in Transition* (Lanham, MD: Rowman and Littlefield, 2013) or any number of Pew Research studies on modern Catholic practice, such as this one: "Just one-third of U.S. Catholics agree with their church that Eucharist is body,

of Christ." Just as a bride will adorn and perfume herself before joining the groom for their nuptial feast, so ought we to adorn ourselves, Paul exhorts, with the virtues that beautify the soul. It has long been shown that rates of sexual abuse in the Catholic Church are no higher than those found among other religious denominations, or among public school teachers and coaches; but no one expects school teachers to transform bread and wine or forgive sins. Only priests do these.[3] As the old adage has it, *corruptio optimi pessima est*, the corruption of the best is the worst. Scandal in the Church is always more scandalous.

To this picture of the Church as the "Bride" the Bible adds other images. In chapter 14 of St. Matthew's Gospel we see Jesus retire to the hills in solitude to pray as his disciples travel along the sea without him to Capernaum. Wind and water rise against them, tossing their boat like a cat's toy. Tradition has taken this boat to be an image of the Church's pilgrimage through time. "The waves that agitate the ship," observes St. Augustine, represent "the clamors of revilers." These are a figure of the temptations that the Church suffers because "the love of many waxes cold."[4] As love diminishes, waves increase. And yet, however strong the tempest, however frag-

blood of Christ" (August 5, 2019), www.pewresearch.org/fact-tank/2019/08/05/transubstantiation-eucharist-u-s-catholics.

3. For a judicious treatment of the abuse by clergy, as well as the mainstream media's construction of the problem as a crisis affecting the Catholic Church in particular, see Philip Jenkins, *Pedophiles and Priests: Anatomy of a Contemporary Crisis* (Oxford: Oxford University Press, 2001). Among the most authoritative studies of abuse by Catholic clergy is the 2011 John Jay Report "The Causes and Context of Sexual Abuse of Minors by Catholic Priests in the United States, 1950–2010" (which establishes the figure that 4 percent of priests between 1950–2002 were accused of sexual abuse against a minor, at page 8). For general orientation see Thomas G. Plante's "Separating Facts about Clergy Abuse from Fiction" in *Psychology Today* (August 23, 2018), where he cites US Department of Education research that puts the percentage of public school teachers that have engaged in sexual abuse of students at between 5–7 percent. The U.S Department of Education's 2004 report "Educator Sexual Misconduct: A Synthesis of Existing Literature" (at p. 20) finds that some 9.6 percent of U.S. public school students experience some form of sexual misconduct by school staff.

4. Augustine, *Commentary on the Gospel of John*, Tractate 25.5–6 (trans. Gibb, Nicene and Post-Nicene Fathers).

ile the ship, wind and wave and darkness will never cause the Bride to be diverted from her divinely charted course. So, if the Lord loves his Bride, why does he allow such storms? And, to ask this question with a view to recent scandals: given the height of the waves, is the Church in any condition to project its message into hostile regions, to launch upon rough seas?

This is not an unreasonable worry. The project of the new evangelization presumes a certain stability of doctrine and practice. One neither fishes well nor travels quickly in a boat in danger of capsizing. Alternatively, one might prefer to recast the concept of evangelization into less combative terms. Perhaps the Church of today should be less thought of as an ark, but rather as a sheepfold or "field hospital." In these later images, what the Church needs to offer is not a forward advance, not confrontation, but rather a message of consolation, mercy, and love. Surely, we need both families of images and others.[5] Yet the image of the bride and the boat seem particularly apt for our times. The bride reminds us that we are loved; the boat why we are chastised. St. Thomas Aquinas says that the rising of the waves, mentioned in the Gospel, are allowed ultimately for our good. God permits suffering and scandal to inflict the Church so that "our virtue may be tested."[6] This ancient confidence in the stability of the Church's saving mission—not the intelligence of any one pope or the integrity of particular bishops or the fidelity of any group of lay people—is what Roman Catholics mean by the Church's indefectibility.[7]

II

Only late in life did John Henry Newman gain such confidence. His early view of Rome veered somewhere between relative indifference and fierce hostility. This was typical for Protestants of his place and

5. For a comprehensive list, see *Lumen Gentium*, 1.5.

6. St. Thomas, *Commentary on the Gospel of St. John*, trans. J. A. Weisheipl, O.P. (Albany, NY: Magi Books, 1998), ch. 6, lecture 1, para 880.

7. A theme developed in Newman in *BS*, reproduced in the appendix.

time. The average nineteenth century Briton felt a similar antagonism toward the Church that stridently secular people of today feel toward religion in general. Catholicism didn't well coincide with, as we might say now, the "common values" of British society. The leading elites of Newman's time viewed Catholics as narrowminded, mostly ignorant, and corrupt. As a young man, his own views corresponded to this impression. Even up to his 40s, the poor example of Roman Catholics hindered him from feeling much sympathy with their Church. In one of his letters, he writes with animus to another friend of Rome's need to reform:

> Rome must change first of all in her spirit. I must see more sanctity in her than I do at present. Alas! I see no marks of sanctity.... If they want to convert England, let them go barefooted into our manufacturing towns, let them preach to the people, like St. Francis Xavier, let them be pelted and trampled on....[8]

Newman's plea has not lost its force. We could substitute other saints and other places to draw the same conclusion today. If Catholics want to convert Ohio or Florida or Massachusetts or Alberta... perhaps Newman would still say let some of the preachers go barefooted! Let her clergy preach the Word of God without compromise; let them stop echoing the easy lessons the world already approves and apply the sword of Scripture to those places where our wounds actually fester. Let her people take up the rosary, the Friday fast, the Gospel of the family, and quit the habit of shopping at Walmart on the Sabbath. Some should literally be unshod. But for most of us renewal would mean stripping from ourselves those easy accommodations that have grown up between Christ and the world. Yes, the Gospel should inform how we think about the environment and immigration, but these are matters upon which good people can differ in their prudential determinations. Abortion, euthanasia, and whether grade three classrooms should be encouraging sexual explorations are not. Avery Dulles, a distinguished student of Newman and an American Cardinal, once observed, "the

8. *LD* viii, 42 to J.R. Bloxam (February 23, 1841).

greatest danger facing the Church in our country today is that of an excessive and indiscreet accommodation."[9] As we shall see, sociological data appears to support this judgment.[10]

As Newman recognized, the Church's faith does not rest upon the character of men. But neither will her message be carried forward apart from us. During his Catholic years, Newman continued to meditate upon the mission of the Church in the world. His own deep historical research had acquainted him with the Church's alternating appearance over time and place. Though Providence would see that the gates of Hell does not triumph, this did not spare the Church from tragedies in the past, nor should we expect it to spare us in the present or future.

III

For Newman, the study of history acted as a ballast for his understanding. Since the Reformation, Catholic activity had been suppressed in England. In the aftermath of Henry VIII's defection, some 350 Catholics were martyred for their opposition to the King's claim of supremacy over the Faith. Over the eighteenth and nineteenth centuries a sequence of legislative acts had gradually loosened the noose of persecution from the necks of believers. Two Emancipation Acts of 1778 and 1791 formally legalized Catholic worship. The Catholic Emancipation Act of 1828, introduced in order to avoid an uprising in Ireland, made it legal for Catholics once again to be elected to Parliament. By Newman's time, Catholics in England had long since ceased being martyred—the last execution at Tyburn was in about 1680—but neither could they hold public offices nor organize themselves into regular dioceses. Following the final emancipation act, Pope Pius IX's 1850 papal bull officially

9. See Avery Dulles's brilliant essay, "Catholicism and American Culture: The Uneasy Dialogue," *America*, January 27, 1990, where he outlines strategies for renewing the Church amidst a secular culture—strategies developed within what he calls traditionalist, radical, and neo-conservative stances.

10. See our chapter three for a discussion of this.

restored the Catholic hierarchy in the nation.[11] Once again bishops could actively organize parishes, once again Catholic life in England seemed to rise up from the catacombs.

For the relaunch of the Catholic Church in England its bishops assembled in July 1852 for the Synod of Westminster, at St. Mary's, Oscott. At this grand occasion, the new convert Fr. Newman was asked to preach a homily to the clergy and other gathered dignitaries. The homily he delivered is considered by many his finest. In it he presents a dark picture of the Church in the aftermath of the Reformation and meditates upon the constancy of Providence amidst the changing fortunes of the Church visible.

> So all seemed to be lost; and there was a struggle for a time, and then its priests were cast out or martyred. There were sacrileges innumerable. Its temples were profaned or destroyed; its revenues seized by covetous nobles, or squandered upon the ministers of a new faith. The presence of Catholicism was at length simply removed,—its grace disowned,—its power despised,—its name, except as a matter of history, at length almost unknown. It took a long time to do this thoroughly; much time, much thought, much labour, much expense; but at last it was done. Oh, that miserable day, centuries before we were born! What a martyrdom to live in it and see the fair form of Truth, moral and material, hacked piecemeal, and every limb and organ carried off, and burned in the fire, or cast into the deep! But at last the work was done. Truth was disposed of, and shovelled away, and there was a calm, a silence, a sort of peace;—and such was about the state of things when we were born into this weary world.[12]

Much in these words remains salutary for us. Newman's view of the Church is not "optimistic." God protects Her, God guides Her; He does not shelter Her from every evil within or without. In each era, persecutions may threaten, defections may gather, heresies may rage, enemies may strike; and yet, the Bride remains always the Bride; the ship is never overcome.

11. For background see Sheridan Gilley, *Newman and His Age* (New York: Christian Classics, 1990), 242–45.

12. "Second Spring," Homily 10 in *OS*, 170–71.

A sense of the Church's power to weather time's storms strengthened him against drowning in hopelessness. We need to learn this mental fortitude. For us who live in the era when Twitter feeds from Edmonton to New York to Beijing to Rome can summon hysterical cries to swirl about us at any hour, we need the stability of men like Newman now more than ever. The human frailty of the Church, in his view, is more an argument in favor of her divine constitution than a cause for cynicism. Catholicism is ever new. She is forever surprising her enemies. Protestants in Newman's time, as ours, would often point to the corruption of the sixteenth-century Church as proof that she had lost her way. But in Newman's view, one had only to wait for a Second Spring. As he will remark to a friend in one of his letters, though tempests rage, the Church has ever regained her strength. "Indeed the outburst of Saints in 1500–1600 after the monstrous corruption," he suggests "seems to me one of the great arguments for Christianity. It is the third marvelous phenomenon in its history; the conversion of the Roman Empire, the reaction under Hildebrand, the resurrection under Ignatius, Teresa, Vincent and a host of others."[13]

And so it is for us. We too may, or rather must, look again for the Second Spring. Christ promised that not even the Gates of Hell could prevail. The waves will never overcome the great ark of God. "Duc in altum," put out into the deep for a catch! This was the message of John Paul II at the opening of this third Christian millennium.[14] It is the message also of John Henry Newman to us. Whatever desolations may befall, whatever scandals may erupt, whatever waves may yet rock us, along with Newman we too should remain confident that the Groom will not abandon his Bride.

13. *LD* xxx, 264, to Richard Holt Hutton, October 12, 1883.

14. John Paul II, *Novo Millennio Ineunte, Apostolic Letter at the Close of the Great Jubilee of the Year* 2000 (January 6, 2001), 1.

3

Evangelizing the "Nones"

"Ten thousand difficulties do not make one doubt"[1]

I

Western culture over the past thirty years has seen radical disruptions. Not all of these have been bad. Racism today is everywhere condemned. Believers and unbelievers promote sustainable stewardship. Who could've imagined the wonders of "Bluetooth" technology only years ago? Not all trends have been corrosive. But many have. Though priestly scandals require sustained attention and deep reparation, far more portentous for the Church of the twenty-first century is the rise of the "nones."

For those in the business of tracking popular culture, particularly in North America, this is surely the most astonishing shift in recent years. Sociologists define "nones" as those who claim no religious tradition. Their rise has been swift. Around 1960, for example, some 98 percent of Canadians explicitly identified with either Catholic or Protestant Christianity, while less than 1 percent claimed no religion.[2] In 1971 4 percent ticked the "none" box, and by 2001 that number had risen to 16 percent. Today, both in the United States and Canada, though majorities continue to identify as Christian, some 1 out of 4 in the US identify with none, among Millennials, that figure rises to just under 1 out of 3 (29 percent), and among Generation Z just over 1 out of 3 (34 percent); nones are even more

1. *Apo* v, 239.

2. Reginald Bibby, *Beyond the Gods and Back* (Lethbridge, AB: Project Canada Books, 2011), 9.

numerous in Canada.[3] If the heart has its reasons, as Pascal quipped, young people seem not to be finding them.

This absence of faith correlates to other losses worth tallying. Take the discipline of the Sunday obligation. Today, somewhere between one and two out of ten Catholics show up to Mass, in Canada and the US, respectively.[4] Or consider the arts. One of the glories of Western culture is the way in which Catholic doctrine has ennobled artists' work. Calling to mind Paris's Notre Dame Cathedral—that beloved monument to faith that even secular France recently stood up to rebuild—or Bach's *B-minor Mass*, or Michelangelo's *David*, makes obvious enough this cultural fact. Despite this, since at least the 1960s mainstream European and North America artists have gone out of their way to distance their work from faith, even to mock religion and to desecrate beauty. In the early twentieth century, Marcel Duchamp's *Fountain* (a urinal) was the first clear example of this trend, or you could think of Tracy Emin's celebrated art show *My Bed*, or Cirque du Soleil's Las Vegas extravaganza *Love*, ostensibly an encomium to the Beetles, but as some have pointed out, a not so subtle ridicule of Christian faith.[5] Such works reflect back a sense of cultural fatigue, what the Germans call *Geschichtsmüde*. We wonder whether our history has entered a cul

3. In Canada 34.6 percent are nones, as per the latest census: https://www150.statcan.gc.ca/n1/daily-quotidien/221026/dq221026b-eng.htm. On US and Canadian data, see studies by the Pew Research Center, "Millennials increasingly are driving growth of 'nones'" (May 12, 2015) and "Changing Face of Religion in Canada" (June 27, 2013); Generation X we'll count as aged 41–60, Millennials as 25–40, Generation Z as 18–24 as per the Survey Center on America Life data and report by Daniel A. Cox, "Generation Z and the Future of Faith in America" (March 24, 2022).

4. As of 2022, nine percent of Canada's Catholics attend Mass weekly—although note this difference between young and old: Catholics under forty years of age are "nearly twice as likely as older Roman Catholics to attend religious services once a month (23 percent versus 12 percent)." See Cardus's November 2022 Report *The Shifting Religious Landscape in Canada*, https://www.cardus.ca/research/spirited-citizenship/reports/the-shifting-landscape-of-faith-in-canada/; the latest data from CARA puts seventeen percent of American Catholics as attending weekly: https://cara.georgetown.edu/faqs.

5. Recently bought for 2.54 million pounds: www.theguardian.com/uk-news/2015/mar/30/tracey-emins-messy-bed-displayed-tate-britain-first-time-in-15-years. On Cirque du Soleil, see the commentary in *St Austin Review*, July 2018.

de sac. The beautiful no longer inspires. Truth seems impossibly remote. Contemporary art feels like the play of an abandoned child, lacking in skill as much as it lacks in innocence. A similar weariness weighs upon our moral aspirations. Consider the contemporary transhuman and transgender movements: in government-sanctioned laboratories across the globe, genetic materials from pigs now intermingle with human DNA so as to blur the distinction between man and beast; likewise, in progressive classrooms boys and girls are being encouraged to blur the distinction between girls and boys. Human identity seems everywhere to be reduced to naked acts of will. While the progressive movements of our time have done well to break down barriers, they offer little direction as to what to do with liberated freedom once you've found it.

When trying to shepherd a none toward faith it is helpful to remember that nones are not equivalent to hardened atheists. Most are lapsed Christians, or at least had grandparents and maybe parents who went to church but for whatever reasons did not transmit the habit to their children. At the same time, these nones often carry over sentiments that originally grew out of living faith; they value generosity and openness and equity, say, but have no way of relating the parts of their moral convictions into a coherent whole. And so movements and "causes" have taken the place of faith. Causes are counterfeit religions. They offer some of the benefits without the moral or intellectual obligations that real religions impose upon their members. The Black Lives Matter movement, to take just one example, imparts a community, an orthodoxy, a ritual, a scapegoat, and a promise of redemption. But it can give nothing else. The Woke Awakening, that cluster of causes that parodies America's Great Awakenings of the past, is like a dark cloud that will never burst forth with rain; it has the power perhaps to unite some against perceived injustices, but lacking substance, it has no way of nourishing the communities whose evils they set out to destroy. When you ask nones why they don't belong to a religious tradition, what do they say? Frankly, they often don't know what to say. I've spent my adult life working with college students and when you ask one why he or she has stopped going to church, the first reply is usually ankle deep. When a 21-year-old sleeps in on Sunday it's rarely because he has a problem with the hypostatic union, or because he just can't bring himself to accept Ephesus's declaration of the Blessed Virgin as the *Theotokos*. The confusion typically lies closer to the hips. He's been drifting already for years. He's had a pornography problem since fourteen. As a sophomore at college he moved in with his girlfriend, and now, somehow, St. Joseph's liturgy just doesn't seem compelling. All true enough. Later we will speak to how the liturgy, education, and other cultural habits shape faith; here, drawing from Newman, I'd like to emphasize the vast difference between a genuine *doubt* and a mere, or merely confused, difficulty. Even before charity, it's a matter of simple courtesy. Catholics have a pressing duty to teach: as things stand, most nones have no realistic notion of what it is they claim to reject.

II

Let me pause before proceeding. Since Vatican II some Catholics have acquired a dislike for apologetics. Apologetics is that branch of theology which concerns itself with the defense of the faith. It draws chiefly upon history and philosophy. Not that such argumentation can substitute for revelation. Apologetics helps to show, rather, why it is reasonable to accept the Church's claim to convey and interpret God's mind. It considers and sifts various erroneous views so as to "instill in the hearts of men" both "natural and supernatural truth."[6] As it happens, many who were formed in the early post-Vatican II era came to see apologetics as out of step with the mission of the contemporary Church. When people reject the project of apologetics it is typically for two reasons. One is that trying to persuade people of other religions to become Catholic seems unnecessary, the other, that it is ineffective.

It is worth walking through each objection. The first asserts that, since God is active in other religions and especially among Protestants, we don't need to evangelize them. This argument against apologetics is based on a misunderstanding or a conflation of the

6. Pius XII, *Humani Generis*, in Denzinger 3879.

letter with what has sometimes been labelled the "spirit" of the Council. It is certainly true that elements of grace are active outside of the visible confines of the Catholic Church. Yet these graces *derive from* the Church and are in themselves "calls to 'Catholic unity.'"[7] What is more, as the Council fathers went on to clarify elsewhere, to receive "the fullness of the means of salvation" one must not look to Missouri Synod Lutherans or your neighborhood Bible Church, let alone mosques or temples. The fullness of grace resides in "Christ's Catholic Church alone."[8] Evidently it remains the Lord's hope that all peoples should enter into full communion with his Bride. To cease to defend Catholic truth is consciously to rob souls of ready access to their greatest good. We can say this in other terms. To give up on apologetics would be to withhold from others the opportunity of joining the one true Church, that communion which alone can guarantee "the objective possibility of professing the true faith without error."[9] To withhold such a good is not charitable. It is a sign of spiritual neglect. It is also a mark of "a society of exclusion" against which pope Francis so often warns.[10] Fulton Sheen once observed how some think America "is suffering from intolerance." He did not agree. "It is suffering," rather, "from tolerance: tolerance of right and wrong, truth and error, virtue and evil, Christ and chaos."[11] Although perhaps this liberal tolerance is seeing its final hours. In any case, contrary to a certain sort of ecumenist, even after the last Vatican Council, as the *Catechism* relates, the Church retains her essential "missionary dynamism,"[12] a dynamism served also by apologetics.

The other common reason cited for rejecting apologetics is that it seems ineffective. Religion is chiefly a matter of the heart, it is said, not of the head. Since religion is personal, and since it touches upon

7. *Lumen Gentium* 8, cited in CCC 817.

8. *Unitatis Redintegratio* 3.5, cited in CCC 816.

9. CCC 890, a proclamation which is the particular genius of the Petrine office.

10. Francis, *Fratelli Tutti, On Fraternity and Social Friendship* (2020), 67.

11. Fulton Sheen, *Old Errors and New Labels* (New York: The Century Co., 1931), 95.

12. CCC 851.

regions where argument cannot enter, appeal to reason will be fruitless. This is a more serious objection to the project of apologetics since it comes closer to describing the real limits of reason's reach.

Before we show what is false in this second assertion it is worth noting what is true in it. Newman would surely agree that reason alone can never establish faith. Newman ever promoted the reconciliation of reason and faith, never faith's absorption into reason. Indeed, in his last major work, *The Grammar of Assent,* Newman develops a brilliant and innovative account of the psychology of belief. We assent to a doctrine, he says, because of an *accumulation* of various probabilities. The piety of a grandmother, the kindness of a pastor, the beauty of a sunset, a chance reading of the Gospel, these and a hundred other happenings all work together to shape and inform the mind's grasp of compelling evidence. The mind at work upon both secular and religious questions draws together "antecedent probabilities" whose force moves us personally to assent to some truth.[13] That power by which we make such an assent he names the "illative sense."[14] His own testimony offered a powerful witness to the workings of this sense. With reference to his conversion to the Catholic Church Newman freely confessed, "He who made us has so willed that in mathematics indeed we arrive at certitude by rigid demonstration," whereas in religious enquiry "we arrive at certitude by accumulated probabilities."[15]

Newman goes still further. To prove is not to persuade. Persuasion, the art of moving another's will to assent, requires nearly as many kinds of proofs as there are people. This insight runs throughout Cardinal's long career of thinking about the conditions for belief. And, as an aside, here we meet another fruit that comes from cultivating with Newman *an integrated habit of mind.* Those who have benefited from a liberal education, who have practiced viewing truths in one domain relative to truths in another, are more likely to perceive what different sorts of souls need to hear at different times. To illustrate: some people will be moved more by precept,

13. *GA* part 2, ch. 9, sec. 2.3 and part 2, ch. 10, sec. 2.
14. Ibid., ch. 10, sec. 2.
15. *Apo* v, 199.

others by example, one person by the coherence of the Catholic system, another by seeing the contradictions inherent in their own.

Apologetics is indispensable. Yet it is hardly sufficient. In an early sermon Newman develops this theme, and warns against the folly of too exclusively relying upon argument to secure conversions:

> as regards what are commonly called Evidences, that is, arguments *a posteriori*; conviction for the most part follows, not upon any one great and decisive proof or token of the point in debate, but upon a number of very minute circumstances together, which the mind is quite unable to count up and methodize in an argumentative form.[16]

Apologetics, what he terms "evidences," have a role, though a role that is shared alongside other forms of Christian speech and service. In a late letter Newman reflected with a friend upon the wonders of persuasion. In the movement of the heart, he observed, God grants to us not one proof but many. Before doubts are silenced the seeker needs usually a sequence of converging arguments. He likens this sequence to the cords of a rope. Individual encounters with believers, books, letters, works of art, testimonies, form "a number of separate threads, each feeble, yet together sufficient as an iron rod." He interprets the image:

> An iron rod represents mathematical or strict demonstration; a cable represents moral demonstration, which is an assemblage of probabilities, separately insufficient for certainty, but, when put together, irrefragable. A man who said 'I cannot trust a cable, I must have an iron bar,' would in certain given cases, be irrational and unreasonable: so too is a man who says I must have a rigid demonstration, not moral demonstration, of religious truth.
>
> As such a rope may carry a man, so may such converging strands carry the weight of a man's hope.[17]

All true. Still none of this is an argument *against* apologetics. Indeed, as the heart must find its own reasons, so reason must also

16. *US* Sermon 13 "Implicit and Explicit Reason," para 8.

17. Letter of July 6, 1864 quoted in Wilfred Ward, *The Life of John Henry Cardinal Newman* (London: Longmans Green, 1912), 2:43; on Newman's insight in rela-

quicken the heart. The subtle influences that lead to an interior turn are difficult to trace. Suggestion rises into conviction not usually after a single note has sounded but when a chorus of voices, sometimes singing across lands and years, mysteriously unites into a symphonic harmony whose beauty the soul can no longer resist. In the language of the *Catechism*, philosophical arguments drawn from nature can "predispose one to faith."[18] Newman's own example is again instructive. He sought converts both through the influence of his friendship and the reach of his writings. Consider his books. At various points he worked to show how the presence of miracles, the Church's renewal of culture, and the experience of conscience, each in its own way makes the Catholic faith plausible. On miracles: in Newman's time the philosopher David Hume's (1711–1776) arguments against miracles were felt to be among the strongest; in response to this challenge, early in his career Newman wrote his own *Essay on Miracles*. On culture: as a new Catholic lecturing in Ireland, he marveled in his *Idea of the University* at the Church's power to uphold the moral law against scientists who accept only empirical methods. On conscience: late in life, in his *Grammar of Assent*, he developed an original proof for God based on the interior experience of good and evil, honor and shame.[19] To the question: do we still need apologetics? Newman's reply would be: yes—though we need other modes of persuasion too. Newman would not despair at the apparent unbelief of the nones. They are only waiting for word and witness to come together, like dormant plants in need of the energizing life of both sunshine and rain.

While it is true that evangelizing requires more than argument, neither will it require anything less. Along the course of their forma-

---

tion to the *Catechism* see Petroc Willey's "The Catechism Enshrines the Pedagogy of God," in *Speaking the Truth in Love: The Catechism and the New Evangelization*, Petroc Willey and Scott Sollom, eds. (Steubenville, OH: Emmaus Academic, 2019), 199–218. For orientation to Newman's theory of the justification of religious belief, see Ker, *John Henry Newman: A Biography*, 618–23.

18. CCC 35.

19. On miracles, see *Two Essays on Biblical and on Ecclesiastical Miracles* (1826 and 1843); on the Church's intellectual culture, see *Idea*, 2.4 "Christianity and Medical Science" (1858), on conscience, *GA* part 1, ch. 4, sec. 1 (1870).

tion, young people have been argued out of their faith. We have a duty to argue them back in. Prod a little, or at least prod the more articulate among a young person's friends and you will get a better answer; you may even hear something, eventually, that sounds like an aspirational statement, maybe even something like a manifesto. According to studies, among the most common reasons for leaving church is that nones do not believe in God's existence, and that science makes belief in God impossible.[20] Simply, many young people think faith offends reason. One of the pressing needs of the Church of the twenty-first century, therefore, is to undermine this prejudice.

III

No wonder prejudice abounds. How many under forty could deliver an adult definition of faith? The twentieth-century apologist and bishop, Fulton Sheen, used to say that there are not more than a thousand souls in America that actually reject Catholicism. What most reject are caricatures. In place of genuine faith the market has become flooded with counterfeits. We do well to become familiar with a few of the most popular.[21]

One competing form of faith is a doctrinally liquid Christianity. America has always been a nation of religious entrepreneurs. The nation's first sojourners took refuge here as dissenting Anglicans from across the sea. Nineteenth-century America was the cradle of Emerson and Thoreau's Transcendentalism, of Mary Baker Eddy's

20. See the Pew Study by Becka A. Alper, "Why America's 'nones' don't identify with a religion" (August 8, 2018); when asked what is the most important reason they stay away from religion, the two most commonly cited replies were that they "question a lot of religious teachings" (25 percent) or they "don't believe in God" (22 percent), www.pewresearch.org/fact-tank/2018/08/08/why-americas-nones-dont-identify-with-a-religion; see also the Barna Group's study "Six Reasons Young Christians Leave the Church" (September 27, 2011), www.barna.com/research/six-reasons-young-christians-leave-church.

21. Approaching Newman's thought through the lens of this theme is the object of an admirable study by Reinhard Hütter, *John Henry Newman on Truth and Its Counterfeits: A Guide for Our Times* (Washington, DC: Catholic University of America Press, 2020).

Christian Scientists, of Jehovah's Witnesses, of Mormons, all of whom grew up alongside more historically rooted Baptists, Methodists, Episcopalians and a dozen other denominations. Anti-Catholicism gradually diminished during the twentieth century in America, but the Faith has never held the premier position in public life, as it did, say, in French-speaking Canada. Since World War II it was "mainline" Protestantism mixed with elements from Evangelicalism that provided the moral compass for the better part of the United States.

Such an inheritance is no small achievement. This Biblically oriented, though conceptually malleable public religion helped make possible the assimilation of peoples from every land and creed. It has kept America until now "exceptional." The Founding Fathers, unlike the French Revolutionaries of 1789, did not in general scorn religion. "Of all the dispositions and habits which lead to political prosperity," said George Washington, "religion and morality are indispensable supports. In vain would that man claim the tribute of patriotism, who should labor to subvert these great pillars of human happiness, these firmest props of the duties of men and citizens."[22] When Alexis de Tocqueville, a Catholic aristocrat from France, toured the United States in 1831, he was struck by the deep and pervasive religiosity of America's citizens. At that time he concluded that America is still "the place in the world where the Christian religion has most preserved genuine powers over souls."[23] De Tocqueville grasped well the dynamic between freedom and religion. So did nineteenth-century Americans. Speaking about Catholics in particular, he observed:

> I saw Americans associating to send priests into the new states of the West and to found schools and churches there; they fear that religion will be lost in the woods, and that the people growing up may not be as free as the one from which it has issued.... Thus it

22. Washington's Farewell Address, 1796, www.avalon.law.yale.edu/18th_century/washing.asp.

23. Alexis de Tocqueville, *Democracy in America*, trans. and ed. Harvey C. Mansfield and Delba Winthrop (Chicago: University of Chicago Press, 2000), vol. 1, part 2, ch. 9, 278.

> is that in the United States religious zeal constantly warms itself at the hearth of patriotism.[24]

Freedom thrives only in the soil of self-mastery. Family life, farm life and military life can teach this lesson, but none teaches it better than religion. Citizens of the Republic's first two centuries assumed or at least could assume from others the moral and theological outlook of what we might call *mere* Christianity. When the nation looked to a center, it looked to a form of Protestantism still genetically anchored to the Nicene Creed. And when Americans of even recent decades looked for a national guide, they could find it in someone like Billy Graham, sometime advisor to six presidents.

Today, Protestantism remains the religious glue for the nation. But the formula binds fewer. Another competitor to Catholic faith is a purely therapeutic spirituality. In the twenty-first century, post-doctrinal versions of spirituality have come to occupy or threaten to occupy the new middle. When New York City's Twin Towers were destroyed by terrorists, it was not a pastor that led prayer for the thousands of mourners in Yankee Stadium, but a public entertainer and TV counselor, Oprah Winfrey. A nation of consumers demands a metaphysics that is flexible. Steve Jobs, founder of Apple and a baby boomer spokesperson for the new mood, put it this way: "I think different religions are different doors to the same house. Sometimes I think the house exists, and sometimes I don't. It's the great mystery."[25] A mystery indeed. The contending faith for middle class America is increasingly a religion without creed, without demands, a hardware without software.[26]

Of course Job's dismissal of dogma is hardly daring. In fact, it's lamentably cliché. "Mindfulness" is in, and easy. To seek to be mindful is another way of reaching out to virtue without committing either to the details of a dogma or to the burdens of a duty. We

24. de Tocqueville, *Democracy in America*, vol. 1, part 2, ch. 9, 281.

25. Walter Isaacson, *Steve Jobs* (New York: Simon and Schuster, 2011), 15.

26. See Al Kresta's helpful discussion of these themes in his *Dangers to the Faith: Recognizing Catholicism's Twenty-First Century Opponents* (Huntington, IN: Our Sunday Visitor, 2013).

are passing through an age of moralizing pragmatists. If we take Elizabeth Gilbert, famed author of the thirteen-million-copy *Eat, Pray, Love*, as a representative of this new contentless spirituality, it is little wonder that masses of Millennials who grew up with such mothers don't wish to commit to any "faith." "I think you have every right to cherry-pick when it comes to moving your spirit and finding peace in God." Her counsel brings a lonely comfort. History, dogma, ritual, philosophy, the testimony of the saints, the wisdom of the ages, the authority of popes, the audacity of councils, the clarity of creeds, the devotion of grandmas . . . all of this melts away like a cone of ice cream in the hand of a fourteen-year-old determined to blaze her own path under the afternoon sun. Ms. Gilbert's life offers its own kind of lesson. According to public interviews, since the publication of her manifesto Ms. Gilbert, unfortunately, moved through two marriages, and then switched from desiring romance with men to a more expansive interpretation of her sexual appetites. Returning to metaphysics, she goes on, "I think you are free to search for any metaphor whatsoever which will take you across the worldly divide whenever you need to be transported or comforted. . . . You take whatever works from wherever you can find it, and you keep moving toward the light."[27] With parents like this, whatever religion nones received from their mothers' breasts was more water than milk. Even should "nones" want faith, for what could they be asking?

IV

Contentless religiosity has prepared the soil for the rise of the newly aggressive "Woke" mentality. Newman provides an attractive antidote. He manifests a powerful ability to integrate faith and reason, heart and head, religion and culture. His theology is impeccably orthodox. His definitions are as clear as Aquinas's. His explanations are as ample as Chesterton's. Faith, he tells us, is "an intellectual act,

27. Elizabeth Gilbert, *Eat, Pray, Love*, 10th anniversary ed. (London: Penguin, 2006), 230.

its object truth, and its results knowledge."[28] The epistemic certainty of the object of faith comes not from its inherent probability—as though the doctrine of the Holy Trinity was a lucky guess about God—but from its divine source. Accept once that the Church transmits God's word, and one can believe "because God has spoken," not because one personally "sees its truth and can prove it."[29] Faith, then, has an outside and an inside. There is an objective reality which must be personally appropriated. Even more, it is a gift from above that must at the same time be cultivated in space and time here below. Not that these insights are new. What is novel is Newman's manner of expressing the experience of faith. His formulations and explanations are often wonderfully sensitive to contemporary difficulties.

Here is one example. Better than most others, Newman helps us refine our grasp of the *psychology* of faith. What feelings and mental states attend the mind's trust in God's promises? What does belief feel like from the inside? According to Newman, like living with a body that must age and grow, the life of faith is often painful to endure. Faith is born, grows, expands, and is refined through time. Newman, like many of us, experienced firsthand the anguish of doubt that often accompanies our growth in faith. Though faith is an intellectual act, Newman is clear that it is not the sort of belief that excludes all intellectual or emotional ambiguities. Newman treads on solid ground. A long tradition within the Church speaks freely about God allowing his faithful to suffer through "dark nights" of the soul, as John of the Cross hauntingly described, and as Mother Teresa's life testifies.[30] The dark night refers to the moments of transition between one stage of discipleship and another. As we grow in our trust, the Lord typically removes from us the interior prompts and consolations, the inner sweetness, that formerly we needed to keep us faithful. As we advance, pleasure

28. *Idea*, 1.2.4, "Theology a Branch of Knowledge," 21.

29. DMC, "Faith and Private Judgment."

30. See St. John of the Cross, *Dark Night of the Soul* and Mother Theresa's collection of letters *Come Be My Light* (San Francisco: Ignatius Press, 2015), and, for background, R. Garrigou-Lagrange, *The Three Ages of the Spiritual Life*, 2 vols., trans. Sr. M.T. Doyle (St. Louis, MO: Herder Book Co., 1948).

often diminishes. It is then that the believer is invited to rely less upon the consolations that faith offers than upon the pure will to love. To love even when we don't feel the touch of divine intimacy, to obey even when we don't see directly the reasons—these are a few of the disciplines that the dark night imposes.

But how many nones were ever exposed to such insights? As religious literacy plummeted over the last three decades, so have the number of false impressions concerning faith multiplied. Faith, Newman insists, does not remove all anxieties. When parents or teachers see that a young person encounters deep questions, or what he calls a "difficulty" with the creed, it does not follow that this young person has lost their faith, or that we need to respect their choice against God. Quite the opposite. These for us should usually present an opening for discussion. Often the reasons why young people reject faith are founded upon simple misunderstandings, or confusions, or even false ideas about the kind of certainty that one must attain to abandon the nones and join the ranks of "the religious."

I often go back to a story that a professor of mine told me when I was in college. In his earlier days he had been an atheist, or at least a strident agnostic. It happened one day that in this confident condition of one and twenty he bumped into a religious sister who engaged him in a serious conversation about his lack of faith. He explained his unbelief and explained also to the good nun why it was that he simply could not believe in God. She pressed him a little, prodding him to explain what sort of God it was, precisely, in which he had no faith. My future professor gave his explanation while the nun listened thoughtfully. Once he completed his account she replied, "I think you are correct." And then went on, "I agree with you: the god you don't believe in *doesn't* exist." This nun had internalized Newman's distinction, and it made her a more confident evangelist. His *difficulty* with God had nothing to do with a settled *doubt*. Faith in Christ was not impossible for this young man. But he did need obstacles to be removed. As my professor later would relate the story, this encounter initiated in him something of a change of heart. The prodding of this woman of faith showed him how he knew neither what Christians believe about God nor how they come to hold and maintain their beliefs.

Thousands may reject faith; but millions have never even been given the opportunity. Simply, many people have never been exposed to what it means to *believe* in a Catholic way. When shepherding today's "nones" toward trust in the supernatural, or the claims of the Church, we do well to articulate the difference between real versus apparent obstacles to belief. It is only such an absence within the popular understanding of faith that could make believable, and salable, the sort of wild misrepresentations now commonly leveled against Catholic faith, and not only in the blogosphere. For the atheist biologist Richard Dawkins, faith is "blind trust in the absence of evidence, even in the teeth of evidence" and therefore "evil precisely because it requires no justification, and brooks no argument."[31] Evidently, Dawkins hasn't read much Newman.

In more educated times slurs like this would have been felt too low to warrant a reply.[32] In the words of one of Dawkins's early reviewers, Terry Eagleton, "Imagine someone holding forth on biology whose only knowledge of the subject is the *Book of British Birds*, and you have a rough idea of what it feels like to read Richard Dawkins on theology." Yet Dawkins and other popular atheists have won a wide readership. We need to consider the reasons why. One reason is that millions have had no exposure to a vibrant Catholic culture. Like a generation of bird lovers who have never stepped foot into a real meadow, many of Dawkins's readers, it would appear, have never shared in the thrill of debating real, live, intellectual Christians, or prayed in the midst of the Church's liturgy fully adorned, or eaten a supper with a large family of practicing believers. Instead of such encounters, they too often have had to settle for fairy tale versions of faith, rejecting a doctrine no educated believer holds.

No, for the baptized, adult faith demands much more and much less than your common sceptic would allow. Discipleship requires a

31. Richard Dawkins, *The Selfish Gene*, 30th anniversary edition (Oxford: Oxford University Press, 2006), 198 and *The God Delusion* (Boston: A Mariner Book, 2008), 347.

32. Though replies have, indeed, been offered to Dawkins from all corners of the scholarly world, beginning with Terry Eagleton's delightful review "Lunging, Flailing, Mispunching" in the *London Review of Books* (October 2006).

long renewal of the mind, a wrestling with God like Jacob, and a willingness to ponder like Mary truths which may not at first make obvious sense and yet in time prove true. This is the force of Newman's claim: "Ten thousand difficulties do not make one doubt, as I understand the subject; difficulty and doubt are incommensurate." He continues:

> There of course may be difficulties in the evidence; but I am speaking of difficulties intrinsic to the doctrines themselves, or to their relations with each other. A man may be annoyed that he cannot work out a mathematical problem, of which the answer is or is not given to him, without doubting that it admits of an answer, or that a certain particular answer is the true one. Of all points of faith, the being of a God is, to my own apprehension, encompassed with most difficulty, and yet borne in upon our minds with most power.[33]

One thing is sure: difficulties accompany any adventure. Algebra presents difficulties, chemistry presents difficulties, physics presents difficulties, as does piano, soccer, poetry and every other pursuit worth mastering; still, in none of these domains do we presume that, should a trial arise, should our affections flounder, should our will be opposed, hope would be lost. So also with faith. The Trinity is hard to grasp, Christ's miracles are difficult to prove, God's forgiveness is not easy to accept. In these natural and supernatural pursuits intellectual confidence rests not upon, or not solely upon, one's personal mastery of the subject.

For those who dare to knock, Newman opens doors to inviting rooms. He helps us navigate the inevitable ambiguities that arise from the living struggle to believe. So the first insight we can gain from Newman is this: to find it difficult to hold some Christian teaching is *not equivalent to doubting the faith.* Faith demands the consent of our body, soul, mind, and heart. Although faith is a gift, it is the sort that requires a lifetime to unwrap. We explore next how the right use of the affections can help us take up this work with joy.

33. *Apo* v, 239.

4

Appealing to Affections

"Heart speaks unto heart"[1]

I

Is it possible to hold a dogmatic faith with utter sincerity? Can Christianity satisfy at once both the probing mind and the aching affections? At a high point in his conversion account, Newman describes the state of his thinking since he joined the Church. One of the criticisms levied against Catholics by Newman's contemporaries was that they held doctrines imposed by "a degrading bondage."[2] By this Newman's critics meant that, since Catholicism requires obedience to dogmas, Catholics must appear—in the eyes of the likes of Steve Jobs and the generation of his children—in principle incapable of exercising genuine freedom. Newman reconstructs his objector's view as follows: "The charge is this,"

> that I, as a Catholic, not only make profession to hold doctrines which I cannot possibly believe in my heart, but that I also believe in the existence of a power on earth, which at its own will imposes upon men any new set of *credenda*, when it pleases, by a claim to infallibility; in consequence, that my own thoughts are not my own property. . . .[3]

Before launching into his rebuttal, Newman partially agrees with his detractors. Religious questions, starting with the question of

1. The motto Newman chose as cardinal of the Catholic Church; see Newman, *Meditations and Devotions*, ed. Ian Kerr (New York: Paulist Press), 5.
2. *Apo* v, 246.
3. Ibid.

how to prove God's existence, *are* difficult. Newman confessed, for one, that his perception of God's being was as certain to him "as the certainty of my own existence," even while he freely confessed a lack of clarity. Attempts to put the grounds of that certainty into the logical shape were never, he admitted, "to my satisfaction."[4] Nonetheless, he regarded his own faith as sincere. Among his friends, and eventually also among his enemies, Newman was regarded as a man of outstanding integrity.[5] Indeed, like few before him, this man more than most others wished to know what it means to believe with one's whole mind and affections, to cling to and commune with God, as one heart speaks to another, *cor ad cor loquitur.* Later we'll take up Newman's method for resolving potential conflicts between faith and science; here I should like to linger on the positive role of the affections in the life of faith.

II

Faith is an intellectual act. It is an assent to truths revealed. One of the chief errors of Protestantism, according to Newman, and an error often made by "nones," is to think that faith should be accepted or rejected on the basis of feelings. Wrong, and wrong. But mistakes too can instruct. And this one in particular contains within it a seed of truth now as often ignored as it is exaggerated. While faith could never be based upon one's feelings, faith will rarely be personally appropriated unless it engages and satisfies our passions and affections. For Newman affections are essential. It is essential therefore that we cultivate them well.

In one of Newman's homilies he even goes so far as to locate happiness itself with the satisfaction of our affections. He may be overstating his case, but it is worth following the progression of his ideas. The heart, the affections—we'll try to define Newman's sense of the term in a moment—are the very "instruments" by which the soul achieves its own particular pleasure. He writes provocatively:

4. Ibid., 241.

5. See Roderick Strange's observations on Newman's longstanding friendships in *Newman: A Portrait in Letters*, 18–21.

> I say, then, that the happiness of the soul consists in the exercise of the affections; not in sensual pleasures, not in activity, not in excitement, not in self-esteem, not in the consciousness of power, not in knowledge; in none of these things lies our happiness, but in our affections being elicited, employed, supplied. As hunger and thirst, as taste, sound, and smell, are the channels through which this bodily frame receives pleasure, so the affections are the instruments by which the soul has pleasure. When they are exercised duly, it is happy; when they are undeveloped, restrained, or thwarted, it is not happy. This is our real and true bliss, not to know, or to affect, or to pursue; but to love, to hope, to joy, to admire, to revere, to adore. Our real and true bliss lies in the possession of those objects on which our hearts may rest and be satisfied.[6]

Whatever we make of his view of the affections, it must be distinguished from three competitive descriptions. Against one school, Newman separates his use of "affections" from a bodily account of happiness. Happiness is not the same as "sensual pleasure." He is no Epicurean. Against another, neither does happiness consist in the *libido dominandi*, the will to domination or "the consciousness of power." He is no Nietzschean. Against still another school, neither does he equate happiness to a notional grasp of truths merely. That trend in modern philosophy which treats people as talking heads mistakes the head for the whole of man. Happiness is not to be found, he says, "in knowledge." He is no Cartesian.

What then can Newman mean by the affections? Though their expressions are not identical and though some translation is required, I think Newman's analysis here is in essential agreement with the one given by Thomas Aquinas, and that each account can be enriched by the other.[7]

6. *PPS*, Sermon 22 "Thought of God, Stay of the Soul," 315.

7. For instance: Aquinas pays little attention to the *subjective* experience of emotion; Newman talks about it a great deal. As has been noted, when it comes to accounting for emotions, Aquinas's "primary interest is the *metaphysics* of affectivity, and not the experience of affectivity"; for a detailed study of Aquinas's view of emotion, passions, and affections, see Nicholas E. Lombardo O.P., *The Logic of Desire: Aquinas on Emotion* (Washington, DC: Catholic University of America Press, 2011), citation at 247.

Most basically Newman's use of "affections" mirrors Thomas's understanding of the "appetites." First, for St. Thomas, appetites can be well or badly formed. An appetite describes the inclination of one's desire (*inclinatio appetentis*). The appetites lay down the tracks along which intellectual and bodily desires run. Every natural object has within it definite tendencies. Rocks incline to rest upon earth. Squirrels incline to gather acorns. The rational soul likewise is guided by certain instincts. Far from gazing out upon the world with abandoned indifference, humans reach out toward things perceived *as good*. We ache for order. Thomas thinks this accounts for why the appetitive faculty "is calmed" (*in eo quietetur appetitus*) by the sight of beauty—beauty here as order projected in space and time.[8] There is of course a dramatic difference between monkey and man. Merely animal appetite seeks only what instinct urges. Human appetite, by contrast, is partially formed and partially formable. Our appetite follows the patterns of human instinct and inasmuch as that instinct is damaged by concupiscence our instincts too are damaged. But appetite is also shaped by the goods perceived and understood *by reason*. Our freedom can be used to ennoble or debase our instincts. Thus if you reason badly, you will tend to desire improperly. Eating dessert is wonderful. Thinking everybody's dessert belongs to you is gluttonous. Being rational and hence free, we are at least partially responsible for forming our desires. This is why Thomas can speak of the will as a "rational appetite."[9]

A second observation: the right habituation of appetites entails not their suppression but their ordered satisfaction. Our happiness, even our eternal happiness, to some degree depends upon the satisfaction of *bodily* desire. Men may not be monkeys, but neither are

8. St. Thomas, ST I-II, q27 a1 ad 3. See also Jacques Maritain's helpful discussion on the difference between the Thomistic account of emotion or desire, which always includes reason, and the Kantian account, which excludes it, in *Art and Scholasticism and Other Essays*, trans. J.F. Scanlan (Whitefish, MT: Kessinger Publishing), n. 55, 127.

9. Ibid., q8 a1: "*voluntas est appetitus quidam rationalis . . . appetitus nihil aliud est quam inclinatio appetentis in aliquid*" ("The will is a certain rational appetite . . . the appetite is nothing other than the inclination of one's desire toward something").

they angels. We are composite creatures. We consist of body and soul united. Though St. Thomas says that happiness consists in the intellectual vision of God, he is also clear that the intellect and will *along with the body*, that is to say, that the *whole person of man*, must partake in this beatitude at the resurrection.[10] This view of happiness is opposed to the Buddha, to Plato, to Descartes, and to their New Age grandchildren.

Thomas's psychology is complex. The link I wish to build is simple: both Thomas and Newman emphasize the psychological unity of the human person, body and soul, and that to love God fully one must love with every faculty available. Such an integrated view of psychology has implications for practical piety, as Newman was desirous to explore. Newman's distinctive contribution to our thinking about the affections, I believe, is to be found less in the development of a technical vocabulary than in his insightful pastoral applications. I offer one example to illustrate how Newman's thinking about practical piety weaves beautifully into the fabric of the Church's tradition, past and present.

Cor ad cor loquitur, heart speaks unto heart: Newman's own attempt at summarizing his life's work and thought. By choosing the motto at his investiture as cardinal he situates his thought deep in the Biblical tradition. As with his homily we just looked at above (Sermon 22), Newman will speak of the affections at times as synonymous with *the heart*. In Scripture, the heart is the center of a man's will. To see into the heart is to grasp a man's character laid bare. It is to see him for *what he is now*. "As the faces of them that look therein, shine in the water, so the hearts of men are laid open to the wise" (Prov. 27:19).[11] Along these lines, the heart suggests not only a man's present character but what he regards as *most praise-*

10. The vision of God, as vision, is "an act of the intellect" but as a good "is the object of the will" (ST I-II q11 a1 ad 1); further, since man's natural condition is to be united to his body, and final perfection requires possession of a being's original perfection, "it is required therefore for the ultimate happiness of man (*ad ultimam hominis beatitudinem*) that the soul again be united to the body" (*Comp. Theologiae*, 151).

11. Unless otherwise noted, all Scripture is from the Douay-Rheims translation, the version of Scripture common among Catholics during Newman's life.

worthy. So from Jesus: wherever a man's treasure lay, "there is thy heart also" (Mt 6:21). The heart describes in these two images a state and an aspiration, a present reality and a future hope. It is the heart of man that seeks repose in some final destination and the gift of Christ to grant it. St. Paul can hope, for example, that in his children the peace of Christ will "rejoice in your hearts" (Col. 3:15). We become what we love. Knowledge, power, pleasure, are genuine goods. But Newman wishes to unite these into some more comprehensive object, some all-encompassing good, as he says, echoing St. Augustine, "in which our hearts may rest."

Joseph Ratzinger, in his appropriation of Newman's legacy, draws together the traditional Catholic devotion to the Sacred Heart of Jesus and Newman's emphasis on the heart as an image of *the whole man's affection for Christ*. In the Church's devotion, in Newman, "we are explicitly invited to enter into a spirituality involving the senses." This way of approaching the Christian life corresponds "to the bodily nature of the divine-human love of Jesus Christ." It is never intellect versus will versus appetite. The whole person must be united in praise. As the heart is the "hub of all the senses," Ratzinger goes on, so also is it "the place where sense and spirit meet." When seen in the light of these Thomistic, Biblical, and papal sources, Newman's motto—*cor ad cor loquitur*—expresses beautifully how the unity of our affections calls forth a total gift of self-love.[12] The heart is an apt metaphor for Newman because he constantly wishes us to unite what is in danger of being dissected, compartmentalized, separated within characteristically modern modes of thought. Mind, will, body, soul, need to be raised up together in the act of worship.

This integrating habit of mind is commended also in the *Catechism*. At one point in the *Catechism's* description of the Second Commandment of the Decalogue, appeal is made to Newman on the question of the right ordering of affections.[13] Fear and awe, it is asserted, are integral to a Christian's disposition. If I should unex-

12. Joseph Ratzinger, *Behold the Pierced One: An Approach to a Spiritual Christology* (San Francisco: Ignatius Press, 1986), 56.

13. CCC 2144.

pectedly greet my wife walking along the street or at my college, I feel happy. Quite properly, I am surprised by joy. By contrast, if my affections were habitually to remain silent in the face of goodness or beauty, this would be a sign of disorder. And if not disorder, if I were simply to feel sadness at seeing one I loved, presumably this would indicate either that I did not perceive who it was that approached, or that I had failed to grasp the actual nature of our friendship.

It is likewise with God. Happiness as delightful repose is the heart's correct response before its creator. If happiness can be felt in the presence of creatures, how much more should we feel delight in the creator, by meeting God in the beauty of nature, in conversation with a friend, or in the liturgy. Our feelings in this sense can teach us. However imperfectly, our feelings towards the Lord act like a thermometer of our spiritual temperature. They may at times serve as a gauge that measures whether we have truthfully grasped goods in view of Him whom we claim to serve. As the *Catechism* asserts, "The *sense of the sacred* is part of the virtue of religion," and then quotes Newman:

> They are the class of feelings we *should* have—yes, have to an intense degree—if we literally had the sight of Almighty God; therefore they are the class of feelings which we shall have, *if* we realize His presence. In proportion as we believe that He is present, we shall have them; and not to have them, is not to realize, not to believe that He is present.[14]

Faith flows from the intellect and will, but emotions need their due. If we allow our emotional lives to be formed by elements that circle outside the orbit of Christian culture, our responses will correspondingly be malformed. Hollywood is a poor catechist. Rap music disfigures. Video games enslave. Facebook breeds envy, Twitter strife. The mind operating apart from the motions of the heart rarely incites the will to cling to what is good. In addition to clear propositions about the Lord, we need direct experiences of his love, in the sacraments, through friendships, by acts of charity. When we

14. CCC 2144, quoting Newman, *Parochial and Plain Sermons*, 5.2.

place ourselves in God's way, Newman is encouraging us to expect that at some level our affections will mirror back the truth that *we are loved.* This is not to reduce religion to feelings. Nor is it to promise that emotional healing will ever be complete in this life. It is simply to acknowledge that our faith must reach down to our very flesh. We form affections, then they form us. How to shape them well? Newman's considered insights on art and education offer some practical suggestions for the would-be apologist.

III

As Newman understood, historically, and typically, our affective life is best cultivated in the context of Christian liturgy and art. Newman's was a musical soul. He loved to play the violin. He lived through the English renaissance that was the neo-Gothic revival. Indeed, his leadership in the Oxford Movement was at least indirectly instrumental in encouraging the architecture of Pugin, the painting of Holman Hunt, and the workmanship of William Morris.[15] He was attuned to the indispensable service that the arts offer to religion. Painting, sculpture, music, architecture, and the other "high ministers of the Beautiful and the Noble" are, as he reverently named them, the "special attendants and handmaids of Religion." On Gothic architecture, for example, he offers these words of praise:

> For myself, certainly I think that that style which, whatever be its origin, is called Gothic, is endowed with a profound and a commanding beauty, such as no other style possesses with which we are acquainted, and which probably the Church will not see surpassed till it attain to the Celestial City. No other architecture, now used for sacred purposes, seems to be the growth of an idea, whereas the Gothic style is as harmonious and as intellectual as it is graceful.[16]

These enchantresses can't be left to go their own ways. The very

15. For general orientation, see Kenneth Clark's *The Gothic Revival: An Essay in the History of Taste* (London: John Murray, 1975), 150–75.

16. *Idea*, 1.4.7, "Bearing of Other Branches of Knowledge on Theology," 61.

power of the arts to work upon our affections calls forth from the Church vigilant oversight. As scientism is the abuse of knowledge, so artistry—or its absence—can abet the abuse of emotion. The rapturous joy evoked by the soaring lines of the Gothic arch, he warns, should not blind us to the need to guard our hearts from disordered entanglements. The beauty that "is really a divine gift" is meant to enflame our emotions, is intended to inspire the devout imagination, not leave us merely devoted to physical images. For this reason, the Church can never leave the arts to meddle in religion without direction. He insists on this point. Unless religion is "strong on its own ground," the artist might forget his proper place. Docility is required. The musician, painter, or architect who would serve the Church in the arts must ever "make himself its scholar," must "humbly follow the thoughts given him, and must aim at the glory, not of his own gift, but of the Great Giver."[17] In short, insofar as emotion tutors faith, faith must educate the arts.

Newman spoke about the affections as one who knew how to appeal to them. Besides writing theology, Newman was also one of the finest poets during an age of great poets. As a young man he wrote suggestively that Christian revelation requires that we acquire "a poetical view of things." This is a phrase worth pondering. Revealed religion's tenets, he suggested, "have an originality in them to engage the intellect" all the while its truths and the manner of its disclosures "have a beauty to satisfy the moral nature" of man. A living religion must minister in both directions. It must please mind and sense. He observed, further, that poetry in particular has as its object "the beautiful" and its special office "the gift of moving the affections through the imagination."[18] Music, painting, literature, architecture, each through their sensuous forms, trains the soul to grasp intuitively what is often only later, or not at all, expressed analytically. I may not be able to write a treatise on the glory of God; but when I chant St Thomas Aquinas's *Pange Lingua* during Eucharistic Adoration, or sing Charles Wesley's *Christ the Lord is Risen Today* around the table with my family during Easter, or raise my

17. *Idea*, 1.4.6, "Bearing of Other Branches of Knowledge on Theology," 61.
18. *ECH* "Poetry, with reference to Aristotle's *Poetics*," section 6, 29.

voice with a hundred other worshipers to Newman's *Praise to the Holiest in the Height* while the priest and altar servers arrayed in glittering vestments process up the nave at the beginning of the Mass, all my senses leap into life. And so they ought. As a trumpet becomes fully itself only once breath fills its tubes, so does my flesh and spirit come alive only after I join in the praise of the glory of the Lord. Sings Newman the poet,

> Praise to the Holiest in the height
>   And in the depth be praised;
> In all his words most wonderful,
>   Most sure in all his ways!
>
> O loving wisdom of our God!
>   When all was sin and shame;
> A second Adam to the fight
>   And to the rescue came.[19]

Here is the lesson: causation travels in both directions. Reason's grasp of truth elevates our emotional life. Likewise, the body's encounter with beauty ennobles our understanding.

Newman meditated long upon this two-way interior movement. As we might expect from a thinker who had learned to form an integrated habit of mind, some of Newman's finest insights arise within his imaginative works. For instance, consider a scene from one of his novels, *Loss and Gain: The Story of a Convert.* The story is about a young man's turn to the Catholic Church. In it he recounts the joy of a believer in the act of worship. Our emotional response to the Lord is heightened and enflamed by the drama of the Mass; we may assent to the truths of the faith with our mind, but without experiencing the beauty of the liturgy, without the senses, our grasp would be incomplete. In the course of a believer's practical experience words and arguments sometimes get in the way of communication. They are essential, they are necessary, but they are not sufficient. Concepts bereft of concrete, sensual, sacramental encounters, stumble to convey the beauty of God like the wings of a wounded

19. The verses for the popular hymn "Praise to the Holiest in the Height" originally came from Newman's *Dream of Gerontius.*

goose trying to take flight. It is the mind and body together at prayer in the liturgy, surrounded by incense, nurtured by music, summoned by bells, that gives lift to the wings of our spirit. He lays these words upon the lips of a man coming to know the Church's worship:

> nothing is so consoling, so piercing, so thrilling, so overcoming, as the Mass, said as it is among us. I could attend Masses for ever and not be tired. It is not a mere form of words, —it is a great action, the greatest action that can be on earth. It is, not the invocation merely, but, if I dare use the word, the evocation of the Eternal. He becomes present on the altar in flesh and blood, before whom angels bow and devils tremble. This is that awful event which is the scope, and is the interpretation, of every part of the solemnity. Words are necessary, but as means, not as ends; they are not mere addresses to the throne of grace, they are instruments of what is far higher, of consecration, of sacrifice.[20]

How few nones have encountered worship that could echo this description! From the 1970s on, how impoverished was the architecture of our churches, how silly were our hymns! If you are under 40, unless you've experienced a spiritually privileged upbringing, the culture of Catholicism you encountered was what Newman might have regarded as a beige spirituality, bland and weak.

The choice of Newman's own religious vocation is here also instructive. After his entry to the Church he turned neither to the Benedictines nor to the mendicant preaching orders but to the community that gathered around a saint of the Baroque. Philip Neri (1515–1595), founder of the religious congregation of the Oratorians, lived in an age, as Newman observed, "when literature and art were receiving their fullest development." This joyful missionary of the Counter Reformation did not aim, as did the Puritans, to purify faith from flesh. Instead of lopping off statutes and throwing up whitewashed preaching halls, St. Philip, like St. Ignatius, like St. Charles Borromeo, enlisted the arts in the task of reevangelizing Europe. The Baroque period of the sixteenth and seventeenth centuries above all sought the exaltation of divinized flesh. The fourth

20. *LG* ch. 20, 327–28.

century Church father St. Athanasius had once written that God became man so that man might become God.[21] During the Counter Reformation the Church sanctified art so that art might sanctify man. St. Philip Neri, likewise, was a herald of this revived Christian humanism. He and his Oratorians were eager not to destroy or suppress the arts but "to sanctify poetry, and history, and painting, and music to the glory of the Giver."[22] Newman would surely bid us do the same. If we are to give real assent to revealed truths, the sort of assent that saves, the transformation of our mind and affections will need to go hand and hand.

IV

I should like to take up a last practical matter concerning the affections. I wish to consider how the preacher or Catholic teacher is to engage them. Newman himself was a master of both activities, and most lessons apply to each, though I'll focus on preaching.

Apologetics often unfolds in the context of conversation among friends; nonetheless, at some moments it also figures in the pulpit and the classroom. One of the singular failures of the reform of the last Council fell in the area of homiletics. Anecdotally one often hears that preaching before the Council focused on doctrine whereas preaching after Vatican II has turned our attention to Scripture. Whether the two could ever be sensibly separated is a question we can set aside. How well Catholic homilies engage with Scripture is, however, a matter of concern. An innovative study of some fifty thousand homilies recently published online by churches in the United States revealed some important features about what is said and what is not being said from pulpits. For one thing, Catholic homilies are short. Compared to an average of thirty-nine minutes in Evangelical Protestant Churches, Catholics sit through fourteen minutes of teaching. Now, most Catholics would revolt at a homily longer than, say, twenty minutes. Given that Catholic par-

21. Athanasius, *On the Incarnation*, para 54.
22. *OS*, Sermon 8, "St. Paul's Gift of Sympathy," 119.

ishes generally do not offer a regular fare of Catechism courses or weekly classes on Scripture or doctrine or liturgy to adults, this means the sermon today bears a heavy load. Whether sufficient or not those fourteen minutes have become the all-important verbal means by which to convey the content and spirit of the Church's vision for discipleship. Besides being shorter, some evidence suggests that Catholic homilies may engage less directly with the Bible. In this same study, in 97 percent of the homilies delivered within the Evangelical churches at least one book of the Old or New Testament was named explicitly. In Catholic homilies, by contrast, that number fell to 73 percent. In other words, more than one out of four Catholic homilies didn't mention a book of the Bible at all.[23] What to make of this gap? Perhaps nothing. Or perhaps this at least partially explain why Catholics are about twice as likely to leave their religion than are Evangelicals.[24] In any case, somewhere or somehow Catholic Churches probably need to add to these fourteen minutes of instruction if we are to instill a Catholic mind into our youth.

Whether or not Catholic homilies actually engage less with the Bible, they certainly appear to engage less with the affections of parishioners. In another national study, researchers asked people of different Christian communities what were their reasons for attending or not attending their church. The conclusion: no other group showed less enthusiasm for the sermon than Catholics. Said positively, Catholics who rarely attended church were the *most likely* to report that their primary reason for staying home on Sunday was for the reason that "I don't like the sermons." Again we can draw a contrast. For Catholics, 36 percent said the homily was a "very important" reason for their attendance whereas for Protestants 71

23. The Pew Research Center, "The Digital Pulpit: A Nationwide Analysis of Online Sermons" (December 16, 2019), www.pewforum.org/2019/12/16/the-digital-pulpit-a-nationwide-analysis-of-online-sermons.

24. 21 percent of Americans raised in a Catholic household now identify as "disaffiliated" from their religion compared to only 11 percent of Evangelical Protestants; see the Survey Center on America Life data and report by Daniel A. Cox "Generation Z and the Future of Faith in America" (March 24, 2022), www.americansurveycenter.org/research/generation-z-future-of-faith/#_edn8.

percent said the sermon was a key reason for their attendance.[25] To be sure, Catholics go to Mass for more than the homily. But at Mass, Catholics seek to encounter the Lord through *both* the Table and the Word. There is no coherent theological reason why Catholics shouldn't hope for preaching that is as engaging or as biblically inspired as can be found anywhere else.

How are we to interpret this ambivalence to the contemporary Catholic homily? There are at least two reasons, it seems to me, why the quality of preaching has arguably suffered. One is due to a lack of clarity about the purpose of the homily, the other due to a loss of training in the classical liberal arts, rhetoric in particular.[26] Newman can help on both counts.

What does Newman think the homily is for? He answers simply: "the preacher's object is the spiritual good of his hearer."[27] Following Aristotle, St. Augustine, and St. Francis de Sales, Newman names for the would-be preacher elementary lessons for how to judge which good should be conveyed. Most of all, the preacher must *say something worth hearing*. It is a general truth though still a valuable principle. Newman specifies: the preacher should eschew aiming at relevance; should trust that doctrine is always relevant; should rely not on funny stories to keep attention but the four last things. By these ways will the preacher make clear what the Word of God commands.[28]

But how to do this well? Here is where formation from high school through to college is crucial. The preacher can only draw out

25. The Pew Research Center, "Why Americans Go (and Don't go) to Religious Services" (August 1, 2018), www.pewforum.org/2018/08/01/why-americans-go-to-religious-services.

26. For example, see *Verbum Domini*, fruit of Benedict XVI's Extraordinary Synod on the Word of God, which states that "The homily is a means of bringing the scriptural message to life in a way that helps the faithful to realize that God's word is present and at work in their everyday lives" (para 59). Benedict XVI in that document (60) called for a new *Homiletic Directory*. Subsequently published in 2015 under Francis, it includes a schematic outline which relates the readings of each Sunday to themes treated within the *Catechism of the Catholic Church*.

27. *Idea*, 2.6.2, "University Preaching," 306.

28. Ibid., 2.6.3, 307.

spiritual benefit for his hearers if he has approached Scripture with the aid of the right tools. After the confessional, the intellectual tools most useful to the preacher are forged in the workshop of the classical liberal arts. Newman casts his advice into the idiom of classical rhetoric. To succeed, the preacher must cultivate *ethos*, *logos*, and *pathos*: he must be good, be clear, and attentive. We'll take up his observations on each.

Nothing is more vital than *ethos*. *Ethos* expresses the ethical character and hence moral authority of the speaker. Newman goes further than the classical manuals. He gives a name for the sort of love that must animate the Christian communicator (we might add, of the New Evangelization). He calls it "earnestness." If the preacher is convinced of his message, he will tend to be convincing. If the preacher sees what he wishes to convey, he will be able to show it to us as well. If the preacher understands what he wishes to clarify, he will explain it well. When the preacher believes what he wishes to prove, when he feels what he hopes to impart, when he loves what he wants to make attractive, he will impress far more powerfully than can the most elegant slides using the most colorful images illustrating the simplest of bullet points projected upon the largest of screens in even the most welcoming of softly carpeted sanctuaries. Devotion wins souls. Empty technique repels them. "It is this earnestness," he says, "which is the eloquence of the saints; and not of saints only, but of all Christian preachers."[29]

One more word on *ethos*. Although goodness is the preacher's most important quality, it is also his most difficult accomplishment. The common sense of mankind, Newman reminds us, has once and always determined that "it is safer, where it is possible, to commit oneself to the judgment of men of character than to any considerations addressed merely to the feelings or to the reason."[30] Thus for the preacher virtue comes first. Clergy need time to build credibility. If the people do not trust them, they will not be moved by them. Seminary formation must impart many skills to future pastors. But the "one needful thing" for them remains the same as what it was

29. Ibid.
30. Ibid., 306.

for Martha and Mary (Lk 10:42). Anyone who would preach or teach must become a contemplative in the midst of the world. Fidelity to prayer, the sacraments, a rule of life, a generous spirit, these and every normal means of attaining virtue are all paths upon which the grace of God naturally travels.

While earnestness must be caught, other skills can be taught. The liberal arts in particular can immensely improve the preacher's use of *logos*. *Logos*, in Aristotle's terminology, refers to the persuasive quality of logic. A good sermon from this point of view will be clear, will be concise, will be rigorous in its use of terms, definitions, and arguments. On the rhetorical act, Newman offers advice that the age of the internet has only made more urgent, because it has become less widely known. To set out on this task, the preacher must have in view some *definite* object. We can illustrate. Instead of conveying simply "the goodness of heaven," it would be better to impress on the minds of hearers that "heaven is the fullness of every joy that is here experienced only in part." Rather than "we ought to avoid hell," it would be more penetrating to teach that "hell is the eternal torment of losing all the friends you ever loved and that ever loved you." And so on. To convince, you must be vivid; to be vivid you must be specific. Next, he encourages the apostle of the Word to reduce his message to a single proposition. As a sculpture must be hewn from a single mass of stone, so also the sermon should be crafted from a single theme. "Nothing is so fatal to the effect of a sermon," he observes, "as the habit of preaching on three or four subjects at once."[31] Increasing themes diminishes returns. To a seminarian seeking advice he once advised: "sacrifice every thought, however good and clever, which does not tend to bring out your one point, and . . . aim earnestly and supremely to bring home that one point to the minds of your hearers."[32] The lesson: keep focused.

Besides *ethos*, and *logos*, the preacher must finally attend to *pathos*, the aspect of preaching that directly touches the affections. *Pathos* is not easy to define. In English we bump into derivatives in *pathetic* and *pathological*, neither of which provide particularly

31. Ibid., 2.6.3, 309.

32. *Letter* to a Student at Maynooth (March 2, 1868), 428.

helpful connotations. In its Greek root *pathein* means *to suffer.* It is to be affected, and to undergo some change wrought from the outside. When we speak of the "passion" of Christ, for instance, we refer to his *suffering*, to his receptivity, to his being affected by blows delivered. The speaker must therefore ask: What will hammer the hearts of his hearers? What will inflict a wound that heals? We get some sense of what Newman commends by how he affected others. One listener described the experience of hearing Newman's preaching this way:

> The centre from which his power went forth was the pulpit of St. Mary's, with those wonderful afternoon sermons. Sunday after Sunday, year by year, they went on, each continuing and deepening the impression produced by the last. . . . About the service, the most remarkable thing was the beauty, the silver intonation of Mr. Newman's voice as he read the lessons. . . . The delivery had a peculiarity which it took a new hearer some time to get over. Each separate sentence, or at least each short paragraph, was spoken rapidly, but with great clarity of intonation; and then at its close there was a pause lasting for nearly half a minute; then another rapidly but clearly spoken sentence, followed by another pause. It took some time to get over this, but, that once done, the wonderful charm began to dawn on you.[33]

Rhetoric is a "relative art."[34] Proof is one thing, persuasion another. Rhetoric is not relative absolutely, but it is relative to the needs of the listener. Whereas conclusions of a valid syllogism hold anywhere, the art of rhetoric is directed always toward someone, somewhere. This observation still holds in our age of disembodied information. We need not test the themes, approaches, and illustrations of our sermon or catechetical lesson against the tastes of all listeners who might have access to our words through the web; we need keep in front of our eyes only the sheep of *our* flock. This requires we know them well. A university audience is not a business club is not a Catechism of the Good Shepherd class is not a Catholic

33. J.C. Shairp, "Keble," in *Studies in Poetry and Philosophy* (1868), 211, cited in Keith Beaumont, *Blessed John Henry Newman*, 21.

34. *Idea*, 2.6.3, "University Preaching," 309.

Family Life Conference. Newman's advice is to come to know and love your people, to learn and appreciate their problems, their fears, their virtues, their limits. We may summarize Newman's advice to the apologist in this way. To preach well, see something, say something, say it to someone, and say nothing more.

To evangelize, then, is to bring people to experience afresh their "one great need." Pastors and teachers can absorb this lesson. Far from echoing the sentimental optimism of contemporary suburban spirituality, we will reach more by preaching repentance; in place of liturgies drowning in the rhythms of the shopping mall, better to cultivate chant; instead of avoiding death, we ought to teach the four last things. Yet Newman's apologetic, like our own, can never rest there. It longs for more. It probes into what lies beyond the surfaces and shadows. Faith seeks understanding. And so faith always requires more than the affections. While the experience of longing and dread are necessary preambles and accompaniments to faith, the heart ultimately can only love what is also grasped by the mind. And no belief more haunts the modern imagination than the possibility that God does not exist.

5

De-Normalizing Atheism

"there is no medium, in true philosophy, between atheism and Catholicism"[1]

I

To evangelize well, we need to relearn how to reason about our culture *as though God exists*. The problem is that few of us have been taught to think this way. Even where our faith is earnest, seldom is our thinking integrated. Within our post-Christian culture, education, anthropology, science, and law—to name a few domains—mostly proceed as though theology had nothing to teach it. And so, in the Church's efforts at renewal in the next fifty years, among our chief works will be to denormalize public atheism.

Proving God exists is, frankly, not that difficult. Many and vigorous demonstrations have been offered in support of God by such philosophers as Plato, Aristotle, Plotinus, Augustine, Anselm, Thomas, Leibniz, Kant, Paley, and in our own days, Gödel, Swinburn, and Plantinga, among others.[2] When judged from the point of view of the history of ideas and of cultures, few beliefs have won such universal appeal as belief in a creator. On whatever continent you look, from the plains Indians of North America, to the Aborigines

1. *Apo* iv, 198.

2. For orientation to classical and contemporary sources, one might turn to Peter Kreeft and Ronald K. Tacelli's *Handbook of Catholic Apologetics* (San Francisco: Ignatius Press, 1994) or *The Blackwell Companion to Natural Theology*, ed. William Lane Craig and J.P. Moreland (Oxford: Wiley-Blackwell, 2012) or Robert Spitzer's *New Proofs for the Existence of God* (Grand Rapids, MI: W.B Eerdmans, 2010).

of Australia, to the Aztecs and the Greeks and the Chinese and the Egyptians, men since before history have reverenced the gods. In ancient cultures, denying God reflected a degenerate character, a failed intelligence. In the Jewish imagination, for one, the "atheist" was a symbol of human pride more than a system of belief to be debated. The atheist, so the Jews thought, was a man who prefers his own will over and against reality, akin to the sluggard who would sleep through the harvest in September only to wonder why he is hungry in November, and the sort of person whom the Bible laconically calls a "fool."[3]

Atheism as a force in public life is a distinctively modern phenomenon. For those who wish to understand our godless condition, the "problem with atheism is that it is not a problem."[4] Atheism is not so much a doctrine as a denial. Or rather it has become a situation, an atmosphere, a frame of mind that hovers around us like a fog that has rolled in at twilight. Like a fog, atheism has no positive shape beyond the refusal of those forms affirmed by the religious culture it attempts to overwhelm. Newman, like Nietzsche, was among the first to predict its approach. He more than almost any other in the nineteenth century devoted his imperial intellect to halting the progress of the frightful hurricane that was about to disturb our civilization. Little could Newman have seen with his mind's eye the millions of Jews burned inside gas chambers in Auschwitz and other death camps, or babes surgically removed from wombs with the blessing of Supreme Court Justices. These he could not see in detail. What he did predict was a coming conflict. "An evil time is before us. Principles are being adopted as starting points, which contradict what we know to be axioms."[5] In the years after his death, the world and the Church would suffer from a deluge of apostasy.

> As to the prospects of the Church . . . my apprehensions are not new, but above fifty years standing. I have all that time thought

3. See Psalm 14 and Proverbs 26.

4. So observes Fr. Michael J. Buckley in his magisterial account *At the Origins of Modern Atheism* (New Haven, CT: Yale University Press, 1987), 15.

5. *LD* xxiv, 74.

> that a time of wide-spread infidelity was coming, and through all those years the waters have in fact been rising as a deluge. I look for the time, after my life, when only the tops of mountains will be seen like islands in the waste of waters. I speak principally of the Protestant world—but great actions and successes must be achieved by the Catholic leaders, great wisdom as well as courage must be given them from on high, if Holy Church is to be kept safe from this awful calamity, and, though any trial which came upon her would but be temporary, it may be fierce in the extreme while it lasts.[6]

Ideas carry consequences. Newman's message here is that, though few of us think consistently, or at least think consistently for very long, nevertheless, the seeds of certain concepts tend to produce a life and expression of their own. Whereas previous centuries saw Catholics fighting Muslims or sometimes Protestants, in the West's immediate future he predicted the decisive combat would be between Catholicism and atheistic secularism.

II

In 1879, when Newman was nearly in his 80th year, Pope Leo XIII lifted the aged priest, unexpectedly, to the rank of cardinal. The ceremony in Rome provided Newman with an opportunity to reflect on the progress of irreligion during the nineteenth century and to offer a succinct expression of the coming conflict. Newman's brief oration takes its place alongside the company of Pericles's *Funeral Oration*, D'Arcy McGee's *The Separate School Question*, Lincoln's *Gettysburg Address*, and Benedict XVI's *Regensburg Address*. Few statements better mark the transition from the old world to the new than do Newman's at his investiture in Rome:

> Hitherto the civil Power has been Christian. Even in countries separated from the Church, as in my own, the *dictum* was in force, when I was young, that: "Christianity was the law of the land." Now, everywhere that goodly framework of society, which is the

6. *Letter* to Mrs Maskell, January 6, 1877.

> creation of Christianity, is throwing off Christianity. The *dictum* to which I have referred, with a hundred others which followed upon it, is gone, or is going everywhere; and, by the end of the century, unless the Almighty interferes, it will be forgotten. Hitherto, it has been considered that religion alone, with its supernatural sanctions, was strong enough to secure submission of the masses of our population to law and order; now the Philosophers and Politicians are bent on satisfying this problem without the aid of Christianity.[7]

What Newman describes is the turn from the culture of the early Enlightenment, which in English-speaking countries coexisted alongside and depended upon Christianity's moral framework, to the largely post-Christian world of the present, which does not.

Over the course of the past three hundred years even bad men accepted the need for religion within politics. By the end of the nineteenth century, that need was no longer felt or at least not felt as much as it had formerly.[8] New mechanisms of the state sought to replace the old disciplines of religion. Having summed up the momentous turn of his own time, in this same speech he then outlined the practical program for secular reform that in the future he thought would be carried out in the name of public atheism. Consider how prescient was Newman's grasp of this social dynamic that has, in recent decades within both Europe and North America, become normalized:

> Instead of the Church's authority and teaching, they would substitute first of all a universal and a thoroughly secular education, calculated to bring home to every individual that to be orderly, industrious, and sober, is his personal interest. Then, for great working principles to take the place of religion, for the use of the masses thus carefully educated, it provides—the broad fundamental ethical truths, of justice, benevolence, veracity, and the like . . . and those natural laws which exist and act spontaneously in society, and in social matters, whether physical or psychologi-

7. *BS*, included in the appendix.

8. For an admirable study see Owen Chadwick's *The Secularization of the European Mind in the Nineteenth Century* (Cambridge: Cambridge University Press, 1974).

> cal; for instance, in government, trade, finance, sanitary experiments, and the intercourse of nations. As to Religion, it is a private luxury, which a man may have if he will; but which of course he must pay for, and which he must not obtrude upon others, or indulge in to their annoyance.[9]

The eclipse of religion as a public force within culture, Newman suggests, will be achieved chiefly through control of education. Although every aspect of culture will suffer the effects of total renovation, the instruments most essential to this work concern the life of the mind. We'll take up Newman's positive argument for a return to the classical liberal arts in the final chapter; here I observe a few of the shadows that public atheism casts over our intellectual culture.

III

Newman's first prediction in his *Biglietto Speech* concerns the state's incursions into education. The godless state, he avers, will attempt to seize a monopoly over learning. Family and state will face each other in a zero-sum conflict. This new mode of mental and moral formation will supplant the authority of the Church, and in its turn, of the family. Such was the experience of half the globe under communism, and of many parents now that the "free" world has come under the watchful eye of human rights commissions and tribunals. Consider: if with the aid of school administrators your twelve-year-old asks to remove body parts, surgically or chemically, and you voice disapproval, can you be sure the state won't fine you? A generation ago one needed to open the pages of a dystopian novel to find such horrors; now all you need is a newspaper.[10]

The first turn is an affront against subsidiarity. The second opposes the content of justice. In the new order, shifting standards of self-interest will replace a normative doctrine of the good. Within

9. *BS*.

10. See the case A.B. *v* C.D., 2020 BCCA 11 where the British Columbia Supreme Court had ruled that "misgendering" your children (i.e., not referring to them by their chosen pronoun) constituted "family violence" under the Family Law Act, and such conduct was therefore punishable by police interference. The Court

godless education, the old theological terms and virtues, such as charity, will be replaced by mirroring counterparts, like benevolence—or closer to us, "tolerance" and "diversity." We need to be clear about this. Relativism opens the path to a constant revision of our moral vocabulary. In the terms of progressive educationalists, the future is open. As John Dewey (1859–1952), the single most important architect of North American public education, wrote two generations after Newman: "We institute standards of justice, truth, aesthetic quality, etc., exactly as we set up a platinum bar as a standard measure of lengths. The standard is just as much subject to modification and revision in the one case as the other."[11]

The standard is *open to modification*. Those words have a generous and inclusive ring about them. What follows is otherwise. George Orwell's novel *1984* put flesh onto the bones of Dewey's skeleton. The result? In the absence of truth, state power presides over public definitions of family, man, woman, child, and justice. In the terms set out by Orwell, "Newspeak" is displacing frank speech. Mainstream legacy media did not threaten to become post-truth overnight. With the near-monopoly over education has come the imposition of state-sanctioned words. Categories and definitions long cherished within our educational and legal traditions have begun to crumple and fold, sometimes beyond recognition. At the level of law, what is *habeas corpus*, *stare decisis*, free speech, or the simple dignity of a Philippine woman when pitted against the grievances of a transgendered male looking for a Brazilian body wax? Given the postmodern education of our leadership class, who can guess how a human rights judge may adjudicate in such conflicts?[12]

---

of Appeal subsequently overturned this particular ruling, but still issued a "conduct" order, requiring the father to refrain from "misgendering" his child, see para 209–214: www.canlii.org/en/bc/bcca/doc/2020/2020bcca11/2020bcca11.html. For a commentary by one the case's interveners: www.jccf.ca/court_cases/ab-v-cd.

11. John Dewey, *Logic: The Theory of Inquiry* (New York: Henry Holt & Co., 1938), 216.

12. Unfortunately, another reference to life in Supernatural British Columbia: cf. Yaniv v. Various Waxing Salons (No. 2), 2019 BCHRT 222; www.jccf.ca/wp-content/uploads/2019/10/222_Yaniv_v_Various_Waxing_Salons_No_2_2019_BCHRT_222.pdf.

The renovation of language has also afflicted our public schools. For example, the term "social justice" still has purchase. Who could be against it? It's usage among Christians is venerable. In recent decades, though, the same phrase has come to designate a different object with an opposing intention. Where previously social justice described that form of justice that aims at promoting the *common good*, now it often means nearly the opposite.[13] Social Justice in the twenty-first century rests increasingly not on the sturdy foundations of Scripture or the Natural Law or even the Constitutions of liberal democracies but upon the novel conclusions of so-called "Theory." Critical Theory up until a couple of years ago was a name unknown outside of esoteric circles within left-leaning academia. It is a branch off of the trunk of Marxist and post-Nietzschean scholarship first established in the 1930s by members of the Frankfurt School which then began to spread across the humanities after the sexual revolution of the 1960s.[14] Over recent decades it has developed along paths groomed by the French postmodern thinker Michel Foucault (1926–1984)—for some time the most widely cited author in the Humanities.[15] This body of speculation inspired by Foucault that goes by the name of "Theory" makes a series of remarkable assumptions. One is that power is the only or at least the all-dominant motive for human action. Another is that human identity is neither more nor less than a social construction best reduced to racial, sexual, or economic categories. A last is that justice requires the overturning of Western society and its institutions. Not reason and the reconciliation of conflicting views through

13. A decent starting definition: "Society ensures social justice when it provides the conditions that allow associations or individuals to obtain what is their due, according to their nature and their vocation. Social justice is linked to the common good and the exercise of authority" (CCC 1928).

14. For Max Horkheimer's original manifesto of the aims of the Frankfurt School, see his essay "Traditional and Critical Theory" (1937) in *Critical Theory: Selected Essays*, trans. Matthew O'Connell (New York: Continuum, 2002), 188–243; for orientation, one might begin with the *Internet Encyclopedia of Philosophy* entry on "Critical Theory," www.plato.stanford.edu/entries/critical-theory.

15. High praise evidently quantified by metrics supplied by Google Scholar: see www.michel-foucault.com/2019/05/01/highly-cited-researchers-h100-foucault-at-number-1-2019.

democratic consensus but power and the overthrow of regimes through activism is the order of the day.[16]

One gets a sense for how the culture and institutions of liberal democracies are being prepared for overthrow by the sort of literature that is now delivered to the young and those who form them. Under the cloak of "Theory" and presented as the uncontested conclusions of social scientific "research," Marxist and postmodern principles have been warmly welcomed into classrooms and into highly compensated Professional Development workshops for schoolteachers and corporate leaders across North America. To take but one example, Robin DiAngelo is a noted diversity trainer who has won renown for coining the term "White Fragility." After a summer of race-riots in 2020, her *White Fragility: Why It's So Hard for White People to Talk About Racism* rose to more than one and a half million sales. In her reckoning, "only whites can be racist." She insists "anti-blackness is foundational to our very identities as white people." Against any appearances to the contrary, America is a nation not committed to equality but rather where "the collective white consciousness" enforces systematic racism so as to keep "people of color" below. Like every other original sin, this crime too calls out for atonement. The path forward is for whites to learn to be "less white" so they can become "less racially oppressive." Amazon, Unilever, and the United Methodist Church among other customers have already benefited from this "training."[17]

What happens when the kids also get it from their teachers? DiAngelo's other recent book is a primer on Social Justice education. Her textbook, *Is Everyone Really Equal?: An Introduction to Key Concepts in Social Justice Education*, is pitched at schoolteachers and upper high school or college students. In it she sets out an entirely new moral vocabulary that she thinks responsible teachers will inte-

16. For an authoritative introduction to Foucault's contribution in particular, see Gilles Deleuze's *Foucault* (Minnesota, MN: University of Minnesota Press, 1988) and Gary Gutting's *Foucault: A Very Short Introduction* (Oxford: Oxford University Press, 2005).

17. Robin DiAngelo, *White Fragility: Why It's So Hard for White People to Talk About Racism* (Boston: Beacon Press, 2018), 22, 91, 150; see also Darel E. Paul's review "Against Racialism" in *First Things* (October 2020).

grate into their courses. The concept of "Social Justice" in particular, she believes, is in need of revision. To make the revolutionary social project clear, and in order to avoid confusion between older accounts of justice, she introduces students to what she calls "critical social justice." Note the prefix. The "critical" part in "Social Justice" aims to separate this word from Christian or classically liberal notions of the term. That word hooks her work to the train of scholarship that follows behind Nietzsche and Foucault. The book is well organized and clearly written. It is also wonderfully simplistic. Short folk tales from the orient and vocabulary lists give the book the feel of a grade 5 catechism. Highly speculative conclusions from the far reaches of postmodern academia are expressed as though carrying all the certainty of the Pythagorean theorem. For example, her glossary of terms declares simply that "gender" identifies *nothing more* than "socially prescribed and enforced roles."[18] One wonders: is the dance really that simple to halt? No sign of worry here about jettisoning ten thousand years of accumulated human wisdom about the sexes, or for that matter of a massive amount of scientific research that has over decades unearthed the deep biological differences between the sexes as manifested not only in the brain but in other organs as well.[19] Alas, in spite of all, to many the cosmic marriage of Male and Female has been annulled at the stroke of a pen by "Theory."

Then there is the category of Social Justice itself. For teachers and their students the old wine needs a new skin. The world that DiAngelo represents to the teachers enlisted in her sensitivity-training

18. See Ozlem Sensoy and Robin DiAngelo, *Is Everyone Really Equal?: An Introduction to Key Concepts in Social Justice Education*, second ed. (New York: Teachers College Press, 2017), 223.

19. For orientation, one might begin with a lively opinion piece by two biologists, Colin M. Wright and Emma N. Hilton, "The Dangerous Denial of Sex," *Wall Street Journal* (February 13, 2020); for a fascinating entry into the medical literature, see Geert J. de Vries and Nancy G. Forger, "Sex differences in the brain: a whole body perspective," in *Biology of Sex Differences* vol. 6, article 15, August 15, 2015, doi: 10.1186/s13293-015-0032-z. On the sociological research surrounding sexual differences and their implications for married life and public hearth, see Maggie Gallagher's now classic study *The Case for Marriage: Why Married People Are Happier, Healthier, and Better-off Financially* (New York: Crown Publishing, 2001).

seminars is not a friendly place. It is a world being strangled by the two arms of absolute scepticism and resolute dogmatism. Here again categories drawn from the Judeo-Christian tradition are retained, but the meanings are revised, and replaced with Marxist assumptions about the nature of power. The book's virtue lies in its clarity. The text's opening chapter unveils the master concept as well as the premises that ground the conclusions. On the moral state of modern North America: inequality is something "deeply embedded in the fabric of society"—and thus children are encouraged to think the foundations of their society corrupt. On why people who want to be good can't see that they are bad: "relations of unequal social power are constantly being enacted at both the micro (individual) and macro (structural) levels"—injustice reigns even when it is invisible. As for a remedy: "develop critical social justice literacy"—thus atonement demands a total reengineering of society.[20]

Of course actual racism is everywhere an evil that requires remedy. But to speak of racism in such terms undermines the (stated) good end desired. For one thing, to say that people of any one race are per definition *racist* rejects the promise of a shared humanity. For another, it encourages the evil that actual racism perpetuates: the treatment of people not first as responsible individuals, but as judged from the point of view of some constructed "collective." What is troubling about these experiments in Marxist pedagogy is not so much that their premises are based on a myopic vision of power. Nor is it the duplicity of applying scathing exercises of criticism against other theories while adopting the most simplistic acts of trust toward one's own. What is most worrying is that, if accepted, these ideas now being popularized lead to the unravelling of human communities. To train people to ascribe "white power," "racism," "sexism," "ageism," "homophobia," and a host of other evils as motivating everyone who disagrees with your theory does not repair trust. It is to render into enemies even those who would seek to be your friends. This is neither just nor particularly social.

20. Ozlem Sensoy and Robin DiAngelo, *Is Everyone Really Equal?*, xx–xxi. For a helpful introduction to the knotted world of Critical Race Theory, see James Lindsay's "Woke Encyclopedia" hosted on his website NewDiscourses.com.

So taken are we by the assumption that power is the master category through which to interpret human relations that even if one has never heard of the *Communist Manifesto* we are tempted to think like party members. Instead of engaging with reasons we reflexively reach for the basest of material causes and interests. When people disagree over big questions, we find it difficult to recognize that other interests or motives outside of power, such as friendship, loyalty, or love might also be in play. Indeed, causes and interests often are factors. But they are not the only factors. And only sometimes are they unequivocally the most important ones. We should be clear: to reduce *all* thinking to one's racial or economic standing is really to stop thinking altogether. That's why the game of calling out "bias" is so fun, and so fruitless. If someone tells you, "That's white privilege," what is left to say? You might say "I'm sorry." Then again you might say "I'm sorry, *it's not my fault*." And just as easily you might reply "I'm sorry, you are only saying that because *you are...*"—then filling in the appropriate racial, sexual, economic or other category. It is a habit that proves difficult to break. Once adopted as a starting point for engaging with the views of others, a neo-Marxist approach leads to the loss of a real distinction between *kinds* of conflict. The actual difference between a verbal disagreement and a punch on the nose comes to look moot when you have given up that reason could ever mediate. Conflicts in speech become received the same way as would attacks of force. This is why increasingly on university campuses to argue a point is to open yourself to the charge that you are making someone else feel "unsafe."[21] In many classrooms at least, no more must we wrestle with unexamined premises, worry about false inferences, or consider ambiguous terms. We just need to name a color.

21. See Greg Lukianoff and Jonathan Haidt's *The Coddling of the American Mind: How Good Intentions and Bad Ideas Are Setting Up a Generation for Failure* (New York, NY: Penguin, 2018). Lukianoff is also president of the Foundation for Individual Rights in Education, which yearly tracks the number of disinvitations to speakers made on campuses because of politically-motivated reasons. Here are their stats: for 2012 twenty-one disinvitations, nine of which were from the political right; for 2022 thirty-two disinvitations, six from the right; see https://www.thefire.org/research-learn/campus-disinvitation-database#campus-disinvitations/.

But the likes of DiAngelo are perhaps as much victims of bad ideas as they are their perpetrators. Those who popularize such ideas are not the ones who come up with them. They are reporters at the scene of an earlier tragedy. The real crimes were inflicted decades or centuries ago by others like Marx or Nietzsche or Dewey or Foucault. When John Dewey declared "We institute standards of justice," more accurately he should have said "*the strong* institute standards of justice." For that is the way of the jungle. Once justice is removed from the reach of reason, once might makes right, whether in your renamed Seattle district or in the nation writ large, decency is strangled, and natural inequalities reassert themselves.[22] Progressive or now "woke" academics bear one kind of responsibility. Those who pay them bear another. Today those who most eagerly finance such ideas are the captains of big capital and Big Data. Today "the strong" are increasingly the likes of the one percent who guide the Silicon Valley; and they vote *en bloc*. Unlike the wealthy of the past, they are not to be limited by natural law; nor are they hindered by a sense of *noblesse oblige*, by the ties of family, nation, or religion. These new powers are *beyond* good and evil. In economic terms they regard themselves as "Anywheres" as opposed to "Somewheres."[23] These Anywheres transcend merely social constraints and what they deem to be artificial prejudice and so have become transnational, transgender, and transhumanist. Relativism contained within the rules of international trade is profitable, by some measures. A "rules-based order" that at the same time obliterates local resistance lubricates the ease of the flow of capital. And so even here some among our economic elite depend upon a semblance of justice, though their principles undermine it.

Newman predicted yet a third consequence for education. The higher academies of the future will assert their autonomy from any influence of the Christian religion. During the twentieth century, at

22. I refer to the so-called Capitol Hill Autonomous Zone (CHAZ), www.lifesitenews.com/news/seattle-rioters-attempt-to-burn-police-alive-inside-precinct-building-as-summer-of-violence-continues.

23. See a thoughtful analysis of these social and economic categories by Stephen Harper in *Right Here, Right Now: Politics and Leadership in the Age of Disruption* (Toronto: Penguin, 2018).

certain moments, as when leading Catholic university presidents signed their 1967 Land O'Lakes declaration of independence from the Catholic hierarchy, this drive has taken institutional expressions.[24] More pervasively, though, what we find repeated within the popular organs of culture and education is the presumption that only science gives us access to facts. Religion and morality are subjective; science alone is truthful. This is a position sometimes called "scientism." Rudolf Carnap, the twentieth-century positivist philosopher, put it this way: "no question is in principle unattainable by science."[25] If the scientific method cannot tell us, *it is not knowable.* Science alone claims our reasonable attention. God, beauty, and virtue are not disproved in the new order; they are simply ignored and rendered publicly irrelevant.

IV

Following from these shifts in education, atheism has likewise distorted our view of anthropology. Quite simply, man has become an enigma to himself. Social, physical, and psychological disciplines have in the name of disciplinary autonomy excluded God from the account of human origins and ends. Since ultimate questions are not open to empirical study, they have been buried under more answerable questions. Despite the dizzying complexity of all that science touches, our consciousness, like the cosmos, is officially born of chance. As the crusading atheist and Nobel winning biologist Francis Crick once asserted, "The ultimate aim of the modern movement in biology is in fact to explain all biology in terms of physics and chemistry."[26] Mind is indeed *nothing but* matter. Once this fact is more widely understood, Crick predicted, the humanis-

24. See discussion on the Land O'Lakes Statement in James Burtchaell, C.S.C., *The Dying of the Light: The Disengagement of Colleges and Universities from Their Christian Churches* (Grand Rapids, MI: William B. Eerdmans, 1998), 715.

25. Rudolf Carnap, *The Logical Structure of the World*, trans. R. George (Chicago, IL: Open Court Press, 2003 [1928]), 297.

26. Francis Crick, *Of Molecules and Men* (Amherst, NY: Prometheus Books, 2004 [1966]), 10.

tic civilization the Church helped form in the West over some 2000 years will collapse. Tomorrow's science, he says, "is going to knock their culture right out from underneath them."[27]

Crick may have been more of a prophet than even he realized. The official organs of secular culture perpetuate a view that nearly every leading scientist of a few generations ago, and still many today, would find absurd: that knowledge is reducible to empirical methods. Could scientism ever be good science? A lengthy discussion in Newman's *The Idea of the University* contemplates just such a question. Knowledge, as Newman conceives it, is as a circle. Since the origin of the cosmos is one, so is all knowledge connected. What may be conceived separately through individual sciences in fact exists interdependently. As each science offers one vista upon the Grand Canyon of being, each science helps complete the view offered by the other. As an aside, this is one reason why liberal education, an education that exposes one to each of the major domains of learning, has been prized by Christians for all centuries (though less in our own). Liberal education provides a student with a *comprehensive* view of the whole of learning. It aims for much more than a career. It helps us see for ourselves the circle of knowledge. It breeds intimate familiarity with the powers of and limits to any one discipline.

We can be more concrete. Consider what follows when the circle is broken. Call to mind an apple. What is required to know one? To approach something resembling a complete understanding even of this simplest of objects actually requires a lot of insight. It would require, in addition to physics and geometry, the insights of biology, of horticulture, and of nutrition, at least if we are to grasp its growth, cultivation, and benefit for man. Notice how even a biologist's detailed insights into the chemical structure of a McIntosh's flesh itself tell us nothing about its purpose within an ecosystem, or whether we ought to alter its genetic makeup, how different cultures have viewed its symbolic value, let alone whether I should add it to my diet. Simply, to see with only one set of spectacles is not to see

27. Ibid., 95.

much. And apples are simple. How much more difficult to comprehend is a creature that can be tempted by one! With the addition of man, mind itself enters into the great circle of the physical creation. To study biology or chemistry or physics, let alone literature or history or economics, blind to the difference that free will makes is to halt the progress of science because it is willfully to block from one's view important facts relevant to one's quest for truth. No doubt diet can affect one's mood. But should we really concede with the materialist that John Paul II was great *because* of his Polish cuisine?

Eliminate the rational soul, wipe out the image of God in man, forget Christian anthropology, and you will certainly have simplified your science. But you will have distorted your study. Crick or Dawkins might be good biologists. They are not wise men. When a scientist comes to consider his own special study to be the "key of everything that takes place" he would of necessity be stumbling into error. And we become fools by following them. Newman helps explain why. The omission of any one science, he insists, is bound to distort "the accuracy and completeness" of our knowledge altogether.[28] Speaking now not of declared atheists, but of those scientists who simply imagine their empirical discipline to contain all that reason can comprehend, Newman concludes: "it would not be his science which was untrue, but his so-called knowledge which was unreal."[29] Let us not allow the barnacle of scientism to cling to the glorious ship of science. To reduce mind to matter is no advance in empirical enquiry. It is merely to miss the distinction between final, formal, and material causes.

Newman takes his critique of scientism a step farther. Not only will removing any one discipline damage the circle. If you drop any science, such as theology, "you cannot keep its place vacant for it." The gap will not remain. The other sciences "close up," he says, and "intrude where they have no right."[30] Newman's prediction was accurate. Theology, metaphysics, and ethics, are today replaced by

28. *Idea*, 1.3.4, "Bearing of Theology on Other Branches of Knowledge," 39.
29. Ibid., 1.3.6, 44.
30. *Idea*, 1.4.2, "Bearing of Other Branches of Knowledge on Theology," 55.

economics, physics, and neurobiology. This goes some distance to account for our post-Christian culture's habit of *reductionism.* Remove God, and love is *nothing but* chemistry; sex is nothing but mechanics; beauty is nothing but taste; managing a pandemic requires nothing but medical competence; indeed, the cosmos is nothing but a heap of whirling dust arising from nothing heading to nowhere. The deformed intellectual habit here is to take a complex phenomenon and reduce it to some simpler, simply material, cause. In a typical public university today, one can study anything from protons to politics. But wide vistas never come into one's view. Sadly, what one can almost never encounter is a reasoned forum for considering how the sciences relate in a unified whole or why for that matter life is worth living. As the Catholic novelist and medical doctor Walker Percy once put it, "Why is it possible to learn more in ten minutes about the Crab Nebula in Taurus, which is 6,000 light-years away, than you presently know about yourself, even though you've been stuck with yourself all your life."[31] Good question. Answer: the circle has been broken.

Before we move on, I wish to make one more observation about the shifting role of language within the law, since this too touches upon what results from an approach to life that denies the creator. The lesson here is that one hardly need be a principled atheist to reason like one in fact. Increasingly, all one needs to suffer is the disadvantage of being formed within public institutions.

V

Rights-talk has become the currency in which we trade ideas about justice and the ordering of the law. Observe how for our contemporaries "women's rights," "human rights," and "the right of autonomy" have become code in international forums for state-sanctioned killing. From the point of view of history this is odd. These

31. Walker Percy, *Lost in the Cosmos: The Last Self-Help Book* (New York: Picador, 1983), 1.

terms all find their origins in Christian philosophy, and yet now are regularly deployed to undermine that view.[32] Consider also how, as high schools turned away from the classical "liberal arts" during the 1950s through the 1970s in favor of utilitarian training, we correspondingly lost, in our public media, the habit of defining terms and, in our conversation, the power to disarm vacuous rhetoric. In other words, as public atheism or, in Newman's terms, liberalism exercised more and more influence over our education, the stable definitions of ethical terms have begun to dissolve, be refitted, and then redeployed against religion.

One example along this line will suffice. In 2018 a private Christian University in Canada, Trinity Western, lost its bid to open a law school. Several provincial law societies across the country had withheld recognizing Trinity's program—rendering it impossible for future graduates to practice in these jurisdictions. The societies withheld approval on the grounds that Trinity's students could not, by definition, represent the public interest. Trinity Western at that time asked all students to sign a "community covenant." This statement invited students and staff alike to live chastely. Members of the University bound themselves to a common code of honor similarly to the way that players on hockey teams bind themselves to a common schedule of discipline, or service clubs to goods like "fraternity," or legal firms its members to codes of upright conduct. Alas, this was too much for the provincial law societies. And a majority of Canada's Supreme Justices concurred. The Court ruled that Canada's multicultural, polymorphous society has room for every body except those bodies that voluntarily abstain from exercising a sexual license.[33] The rally for diversity once again became a weapon to enforce secular uniformity.

32. See Jeremy Geddert, *Hugo Grotius and the Modern Theology of Freedom* (New York: Routledge, 2017); Oliver O'Donovan, *The Ways of Judgment* (Grand Rapids, MI: Eerdmans, 2005); Udi Greenberg, "Radical Orthodoxy and the Rebirth of Christian Opposition to Human Rights" in *Christianity and Human Rights Reconsidered*, ed. Sarah Shortall and Daniel Steinmetz-Jenkins (Cambridge: Cambridge University Press, 2020).

33. For additional commentary on the case, see my "An Attack on Us All" in *Convivium* (June 28, 2018), www.convivium.ca/articles/an-attack-on-all.

I raise this case because the legal arguments used to justify the suppression of one Christian University illustrate well Cardinal Newman's observation on the more general effects of public atheism on culture. In the godless, liberal and perhaps postliberal state, Christian capital remains to be spent. But the currency is revalued. Old words that carry the gravitas of tradition and centuries of revered usage are reminted into other tokens. The reassignments will not at first be evident. To say this in other words, the meanings of terms within a counterfeit culture break down the semantic web established under the former dispensation to achieve newly desired ends. Words become weapons. Indeed, the dissenting Justices of the Canadian Supreme Court charged the majority precisely with manipulating the language of the law:

> Charter [of Rights] values like "equality," "justice," and "dignity" become mere rhetorical devices by which courts can give priority to particular moral judgments, under the guise of undefined "values," over other values and over Charter rights themselves.[34]

In denying God, public atheism blocks access to human ends. Yet communities require some account of the human good and in practice are sustained around common loves. Since atheism cannot of itself justify an account of objective justice, it is forced to manufacture counterfeit replicas in the disguised factories of speech.

Is there not some good that has emerged within postrevolutionary politics? Newman would affirm that there was. The secular, liberal tradition of politics contains much that is worth preserving. North America is not yet China. Doctors in most jurisdictions are not yet forced to euthanize patients. In religious controversies against faithful Anglicans, as against secularizing Protestants, Newman was an even-handed crusader.[35] In one of his early poems,

34. TWU *v* Law Society of BC, 2018, SCC 32, dissent of Justices Côté and Brown, para 309.

35. Newman was criticized by some Catholics of the day, for instance, for commending some features of the Anglican communion in his *Apologia*. In a letter to his former Oxford pupil, friend, and Catholic convert, Henry W. Wilberforce (son of the Wilberforce who helped abolish slavery), Newman explains something of his mature mind on the matter. Newman says he is "impatient at" and rejects as an

"Liberalism," he wrote with some generosity of those who had defected from the Gospel to the good news of a secular salvation,

> And ye have caught some echoes of its lore,
> As heralded amid the joyous choirs;
> Ye mark'd it spoke of peace, chastised desires,
> Good-will and mercy,—and ye heard no more.

Secularized Christians, the poem goes on, "halve the Truth," having no more and no less.[36] Almost five decades later, even at the moment of his exaltation over the great enemy, Liberalism (with a capital L), during his *Biglietto* speech before his Roman and papal audience Newman was quick to point out liberalism's genuine virtues. There is much in the classically liberal account of the state and civil society, he will go on, "which is good and true." At its best, liberalism carries forward fragments of the Christian inheritance of "justice, truthfulness, sobriety." And yet, it is this mixing of the Christian with the anti-Christian that is insidious. The partial health of the contagion makes it difficult to inoculate against. It is only after the precepts of religion and the natural law are abrogated, Newman insists, that we declare political liberalism "to be evil."[37] And successfully denormalizing atheism requires that we do indeed name those evils where they arise.

"evil delusion" the notion that an institution, though it be in fundamental error (such as the Anglican communion), cannot yet possess some real measure of greatness: "till we [Catholics] allow that there are greater natural gifts and human works in the Protestant world of England than in the little Catholic flock, we only make ourselves ridiculous and hurt that just inference by which alone we can hope to convert men. If there were no such thing as absolute truth in religious matters, there is great wisdom in a compromise and comprehension of opinions,—and this the Church of England exhibits." In Letter of August 24, 1864, quoted in Ward, *The Life of John Henry Cardinal Newman*, 2:45.

36. *VV*, 'Liberalism' (written 1833), 144–45.

37. *BA*. For insightful observations along these lines, see also Patrick Deneen's *Why Liberalism Failed* (New Haven, CT: Yale University Press, 2018).

VI

Jesus asked once whether we will have mammon or God; Newman asks whether we will take atheism or the Catholic Church. In Newman's estimation, two systems of thought carry such force that by their potency lesser systems will, over time, tend to capitulate towards one or the other. In his own pilgrimage he arrived at a fork in the road. "I came to the conclusion," he confessed, "that there was no medium, in true philosophy, between Atheism and Catholicity" and that a perfectly consistent mind "must embrace either the one or the other."[38] He observed that today, outside of the Catholic Church, things are tending "from the circumstance of the age," to public atheism "in one shape or another."[39]

Such a stark choice could seem simplistic. And perhaps it is. But I note that Newman was not the only observer of his age to anticipate such a future. The first great sociological study of the United States was Alexis de Tocqueville's *Democracy in America*. Like Newman, this Frenchman also predicted that the people of the United States, and indeed of other Western nations, would in religion likely tend towards one of two extreme positions. "I am brought to believe," de Tocqueville concluded, that "our descendants will tend more and more to be divided into only two parts, those leaving Christianity entirely and others entering into the bosom of the Roman Church."[40] Democratic regimes, he reasoned, inculcate a love of equality. Most religions distinguish between the high and the low, the elect and the lost. But by habituation citizens of democratic regimes are naturally suspicious of hierarchies. Hence, from one quarter, democracy encourages secularism. Of course not all social dynamics work against religion. Insofar as religion is acknowledged, democratic peoples will incline toward an authority that is uniform and universal. As the reasoning goes, since all men are equal, *if* there is an authority, that authority should be equally applicable to all. Hence, from another quarter, democracy encourages Catholicism.

38. *Apo* iv, 198.
39. *Apo* v, 244.
40. Tocqueville, *Democracy in America*, vol 2, part 1, ch. 6, 425.

Where de Tocqueville appeals to sociological reasons, Newman's are epistemological. During his life, some took him to assert that the truth of Catholicism follows, necessarily, once atheism is called into doubt. This was not his meaning. What he affirmed, rather, is that once atheism can be set aside, once dogmatic scepticism can be doubted, mocked, denormalized, the hardest hurdle to faith will have been overcome. A royal gate is opened for the mind which formerly had been closed to all explorations. He explains:

> If I must submit my reason to mysteries, it is not much matter whether it is a mystery more or a mystery less; the main difficulty is to believe at all; the main difficulty for an inquirer is firmly to hold that there is a living God, in spite of the darkness which surrounds Him, the Creator, Witness, and Judge of men.[41]

Once the back of atheism is broken, no longer does the "proud, self-sufficient spirit" of unaided human reason regard itself as master of the cosmos. Evidence formerly neglected can for the first time see daylight. The small and great indications of miracles, of self-sacrificial love, of prophesy, of final causality, as well as of the soul's longing for eternal life will rise up before the mind's eye without principled rejection. C.S. Lewis (1898–1963), a famous convert from atheism, himself described this experience as a sort of "melting" away of his formerly protective coat. His armor of unbelief turned out to be no more solid than ice. Once the great thaw began, once faith in a godless cosmos cracked, he could not predict who else would prove a messenger of the spring: "Plato, Dante, MacDonald, Herbert, Barfield, Tolkien, Dyson, Joy itself. Everyone and everything had joined the other side." Lewis goes on:

> The real terror was that if you seriously believed in even such a "God" or "Spirit" as I admitted, a wholly new situation developed. As the dry bones shook and came together in that dreadful valley of Ezekiel's, so now a philosophical theorem, cerebrally entertained, began to stir and heave and throw off its grave cloths, and

41. *GA* notes sec. 2, 497–98.

> stood upright and became a living presence. I was allowed to play at philosophy no longer.[42]

Accept God, and reason must make room for the possibility of faith; admit a creator acts once, and why may he not intervene a hundred times more; and if God be interested in the destiny of men, why might he not become one of us, and call us to become one with him? These are the sorts of questions that evangelists working within the post-Christian West must lift before our eyes.

Even though the religious landscape has altered in ways that Newman could not have anticipated, he was right in this: secularism, fueled by a practical atheism, remains the Church's great threat. By the unabashed exercise of the liturgy, by catechesis, and by an intensified discipleship in the family, and perhaps most of all, by manifesting *the inherent compatibility* of faith and reason in every domain of life—from education to anthropology to law—the Church will indeed need to rebuild the foundations of Catholic culture. Regaining influence within the public sphere will entail denormalizing atheism. Toward that end, the next two chapters consider some practical strategies, the first of which is to name secularism's founding myths.

42. C.S. Lewis, *Surprised by Joy*, near the end of chapter 14, in *C.S. Lewis: Selected Books* (London: Harper Collins, 1999), 1374–75.

6

Three Myths of Secularism

"without the aid of Christianity..."[1]

I

Three foundational myths of the modern imagination have been used more often than others to justify the rejection of religion from public life. The first is that religion breeds violence, the second that science conflicts with faith, the third, which we'll explore in the next chapter, that dignity requires absolute autonomy. These myths undermine the credibility of the Church's evangelical proclamation, and can at least somewhat be demystified with Newman's aid.

The process of secularization arose in the West partially in response to Europe's wars of religion. Between roughly 1520 and 1648 some five thousand judicial executions were ordered in the name of religious orthodoxy, Protestant and Catholic. Even though the conflicts between Catholics and Henry VIII in England, William of Orange in Holland, the Huguenots in France, the Schmalkaldic League in Germany, and between Protestants among themselves were fought over more than simply religious interests, the outcome for Western Christianity was disastrous. Christianity remained the dominant cultural force well into the early modern period. Its legacy, however, was poisoned. The Reformation era's violence continues to this day to serve as a rationale for institutionalized secularism.

One of the unforeseen consequences of the Protestant Reformation was the gradual ejection of religion from politics. The wars of

1. *BS*.

religion bred cynicism even among some who had no wish to deny their faith. "What I consider wrong," observed Montaigne, "is our usual practice of trying to support and confirm our religion by the success or happy outcome of our undertakings." He was talking about the outcomes of wars. Montaigne wrote this in 1571 with a view to the victory only months before at the battle of Lepanto of the Christian fleet over the Moors; he could stand by this judgment a few years later when the Protestant English fleet defeated the Spanish Armada in 1588.[2] Montaigne died a loyal Catholic. But having lived through these conflicts he had grown sceptical about appeals to conquest as evidence for the faith. Others would follow in his steps. More than that, religion would gradually be singled out as though disagreement over doctrine were the sole engine behind sixteenth-century violence.

This is almost certainly not true. Purportedly Christian monarchs in Europe had long fought to increase the reach of their realms. During the eleventh and twelve centuries, at the height of the investiture controversy, German Catholic princes waged a near continual war against popes. Again, for two centuries prior to Luther, during the so-called "Hundred Years' War," the leading dynasties in Europe conducted ever-expanding conflicts in France in the effort to consolidate their claims to inheritance. During the sixteenth century, economic interests also loomed large. When Henry VIII dissolved the monasteries in England it is estimated that he acquired at a stroke some twenty percent of the countryside. The simple truth is that Europeans fought before the Reformation and they continued to fight long after the Reformation. This is not to say that ideas do not matter. It is only to notice that the way we came to narrate the early modern "wars of religion" was not the only way the story could have been told. It is plausible, for one, that the rise of the nation-state could be better described as a *contributing* cause to the Reformation era's violence. In fact, much violence of the so-

2. At the least he saw no need for revision when his essay was reworked some twenty years later a final time, just months after this later Catholic defeat. See Montaigne's "Judgements on God's ordinances must be embarked upon with prudence," in *The Essays: A Selection*, trans. M.A. Screech (London: Penguin, 2004), 94.

called wars of religion might be better explained "in terms of the resistance of local elites to the state-building efforts of monarchs and emperors."[3] In this view it is more the newly emerging national state than "religion" that is to blame.

In any case, identifying the genesis of historical events is always tricky work. And from one point of view it matters little. Wherever we now place the greater causal force, beginning in 1651 with Thomas Hobbes's *Leviathan*, the West's major political philosophers from Locke to Voltaire to Kant, and increasingly its statesmen, made vast rhetorical use of these conflicts. Two centuries of political thinkers repeatedly recalled inter-Christian warfare as a justification for wresting force from the hands of the churches so as to consolidate it within the grip of the nation-state. Civil tranquility required a new monopoly on violence. Argument and persuasion had been as little effective at reconciling theological conflicts as had been the sword. And the state, if it was to contain violence, could no longer look to religion as the arbiter and interpreter of justice. Peace, so the claim went, demanded public scepticism.[4]

If the pastors of the Reformation rejected Catholic orthodoxy in the name of Scripture, the philosophers of the Enlightenment rejected revelation in the name of autonomous reason. The high promise of the Enlightenment predicted that as science and democracy advanced, with peace in its wake, religion would recede, or at least lose its teeth. Said that crusading materialist and *philosophe* Paul-Henry d'Holbach in 1770: "If the ignorance of nature gave birth to such a variety of gods, the knowledge of nature is calculated to destroy them."[5] It was a novel idea to think that science should encourage atheism. Outside of France rarely was God outright denied. Progress was measured more in terms of the expanse of rea-

3. On this, see William T. Cavanaugh's *Myth of Religious Violence: Secular Ideology and the Roots of Modern Conflict* (Oxford: OUP, 2009), 163.

4. See further Brad Gregory's discussion in *The Unintended Reformation: How a Religious Revolution Secularized Society* (Cambridge, MA: The Belknap Press, 2012), 158–62.

5. Paul-Henry d'Holbach, *The System of Nature* (1770), vol 2, trans. by Samuel Wilkinson (Gutenberg ebook, 2005), final lines of chapter one; see commentary by Buckley, *At the Origins of Modern Atheism*, 295.

son and freedom, and of toleration. God could stay. It is only the religious authorities who spoke for him that needed to melt into the distance. The individual was accountable for his conscience to God, and only to God. It is to argue for this conclusion that Thomas Jefferson in America could quip in 1788, "It does me no injury for my neighbor to say there are twenty gods, or no god. It neither picks my pocket nor breaks my leg."[6]

Once the right to be irreligious was conceded, all the institutions needed to adjust, at least theoretically. What was left of the common good tended to become concentrated upon the interests of the individual. Those working within the political tradition that came to be called "liberalism" came to celebrate the right of conscience, as J.S. Mill did, as the very precondition for liberty. Conscience was the one still small point of moral certainty against not only religious interference but also the coercive power of the state. By the nineteenth century the myth of religious violence had been eclipsed in other places by another story. Thinkers in Germany, among them Fichte, Clausewitz, and Hegel, came to regard war as a good necessary to the cleansing of the international order. War is purgative. Conflict keeps nations healthy. Battles restore civic health "as the motion of the winds keeps the sea from stagnation," encouraged Hegel in 1821.[7] During Newman's life, competing with the myth of religious violence was the actual and increasing violence of the nation-state. Liberalism came to see itself as a liberator from both. In this light perhaps it was inevitable that liberalism should celebrate what we now label *individualism*. The forces of religion *and* of the state needed to be kept in check; otherwise the individual would be drowned. In 1859 J.S. Mill would conclude abruptly: so long as one man's liberty does not inhibit another's, "the individual is sovereign."[8]

We are simplifying the story. Yet it remains true that conflict among Christians five centuries ago helped pave a path to the mal-

6. Thomas Jefferson, *Notes on the State of Virginia* (Philadelphia: Prichard and Hall, 1788), ch. 17, 169.

7. Hegel, *Groundwork in the Philosophy of Right* (1821), para 324, cited by Owen Chadwick, *The Secularization of the European Mind in the Nineteenth Century*, 132–33.

8. J.S. Mill, *On Liberty* (London: Penguin, 1985 [1859]), 69.

aise of our present. Should I go to church or join a running club on Sunday? Should I marry or remain single into my 30s? Should society censure me if I choose not to have children? What if I demand you help kill me? The official line has been that public reason *should not judge*. Thus presented the outer face of the post-World War II liberal order of the West. What kind of order appears after the last vestiges of Christianity are formally excised is not likely to be as tolerant.

II

Textbooks often describe the eighteenth century as the "age of reason." This is inaccurate. Reason, by the Enlightenment, had lost its metaphysical reach. It was demoted from its formerly exalted position as a secure link to the divine, a view developed within Greek and Christian philosophy, to become a lowly servant of the passions. Despite the desperate attempts of the nineteenth-century Romantics to find in intuition and emotion and the state what could no longer be hoped for from metaphysics or religion, our concept of "reason" today survives as little more than what David Hume and J.S. Mill (along with Karl Marx) and their intellectual heirs say it is: a tool. And so paradoxically what started out as a desire to tame religion ended up by trapping reason.

With the loss of religion went the promise of a metaphysically ambitious reason. "Big picture" ideas are now rarely welcome in public. When John Rawls (1921–2002)—among the most persuasive contemporary spokesmen for this liberal tradition—recommends to us how citizens are to understand the role of reason, we are told to mind our manners. Our concept of "Reason," he says, should be constructed without "any public controversial elements."[9] Justice as fairness is a matter of procedure. Politicians imbibe this rule. Speaking in public, or at least being taken seriously when speaking in public, requires that we each put on a mask. Fairness arises as long

9. Rawls, *A Theory of Justice*, original ed. (Cambridge, MA: Harvard University Press, 1971), 14. It should be noted that Rawls's later work shows more openness to the public place of religious arguments. On this, see his *Political Liberalism*, expanded edition, 463.

as we restrain from making appeals to metaphysical or ethical principles that other citizens may not accept as reasonable. Such was the liberal secular political orthodoxy between 1780 and 1980.

Today such a strictly policed division between private and public is breaking apart. So is the consensus of so-called liberal secular values. "Public reason" on this account would have us refrain from speaking not only about God, but about killing by doctors, about marriage, about immigration, or about whether it is fair for seventeen-year-old biological males to compete in "all female" racing, running, and swimming competitions with seventeen-year-old girls. Secular North Americans like Western Europeans had gotten used to the idea that rights-talk was universal. The move from human rights, to women's rights, to gay rights, to trans-rights was thought by educated opinion to be nothing else than the unfolding logic of social progress.[10] The painful truth is that it is not.

Western Europeans have been for a time seeing this fact up close. Since the 1970s Europe has pursued a nearly-open-doors policy on immigration. The hope had been that by simply living on the same land the out-of-continent guests would embrace the same liberal, progressive, and supposedly universal values as the hosts. It took decades to recognize the presumption in this view. Now it has become clear that those same values have not been universally embraced. A study in 2009, for instance, found that out of a sample of 500, exactly zero of these British Muslims surveyed thought homosexuality was morally acceptable. Since 2015 millions more North Africans have flooded their continent. Whether Europe will be able to "integrate" this newest wave is still a question. Whether the Muslims who have stepped upon their shores carry their same progressive instincts is not. Another survey on British opinions on homosexuality was carried out in 2015. Presumably, what the researchers thought they would find would be a few backward corners left on the Island not yet reconciled to the progressive multiculturalism of the big cities. What they discovered was just the

10. I call to the witness stand Michael Ignatieff, some-time academic and one time leader of the federal Liberal Party of Canada: see his *The Rights Revolution* (Toronto: House of Anansi Press, 2000).

opposite. Whereas in the country as a whole only 16 percent of Brits thought homosexuality a problem, in London—a city with a large immigrant population—the percentage was nearly double at 29 percent. Who would have thought twenty-five years ago that Britain's largest city would be the country's hold-out against gay rights?[11] Then again twenty-five years ago who would have thought that more people in Britain might soon be weekly attending mosques rather than churches?

Back in North America, rumblings of a breakup of the liberal consensus have been felt in recent years less because of Islamic immigration than because of the rise of so-called "woke" culture. To be "woke" is to have been awakened to systemic injustices. It is to see evils that were everywhere present but nowhere acknowledged. It is often a mark of social prestige. To participate in this new knowledge is to separate oneself from the less morally attuned crowd. And those who are "woke" regard those outside of their circle with deep moral dismay. Whatever else the woke movement portends, it illustrates how little remains of our common ground. And note that all of this is even before one calculates the sum cultural effect of Brexit, Trump, COVID-19, Black Lives Matter, Canada's Freedom Convoy and the US Supreme Court's dazzling 2022 rout of Roe *v* Wade.

III

In the Anglo-American sphere, the common law's notion of the *reasonable man* is one of those monumental achievements of our civilization. Who can now say what stands for "reasonable"? As with other public monuments to our past, secular politics seems unable to resist those who wish to knock down the statues. Those who have embraced the likes of Critical Race Theory urge us to cast aside the old restraints that helped liberal democracies negotiate differences. The rules surrounding decent speech, for one, can so quickly shift

11. "Muslims in Britain have zero tolerance of homosexuality, says poll," *The Guardian*, May 7, 2009 and YouGov survey, fieldwork, February 23–24, 2015, both cited in Douglas Murray's *The Strange Death of Europe: Immigration, Identity, Islam*, updated ed. (London: Bloomsbury, 2019), 54–55.

that even the most accomplished public persons can find it impossible to satisfy the censors. Terms of debate can veer literally at a moment's notice. A poignant instance of this was offered during the 2020 nomination hearings for the (now) US Supreme Court Judge Amy Barrett.[12] During the course of the confirmation hearings, a Senator from Hawaii took issue with Barrett's use of the term "sexual preference" to describe the dispositions of members belonging to the LGTBQ etc. community. The Senator registered her offence. Barrett clarified. She did not use the phrase as a term of disrespect. Unappeased, the Senator insisted Barrett's language *was* inflammatory. One could be forgiven for sympathizing with the judge. It was later discovered that only hours after Barrett's remarks went viral on the web the editors at Merriam-Webster decided to change the definition of "sexual preference" on their online dictionary to explain that this term is "offensive." Not everyone can be blessed with this Senator's premonitions.

Power is coming to be viewed as the real basis of politics. And increasingly all means are on the table to get it.[13] The new left no longer regards religious liberty as sacred. Nor does it feel protective about free speech. Nor is it willing to concede the identity of individuals. This is because the new, new left has embraced the Marxist and postmodern account of identity politics, that is, the view that people are best identified according to the interests of their materially or racially or sexually identified *group*. Unlike during the 1960s, respectable people of all stripes think the new, *new* Left is right. Or at least a near majority doesn't know why they are wrong. This has thrown up for us innumerable difficulties in law. It also rubs against what classical liberals used to take as their first principle: rights adhere first in *individuals*. As even so strident a representative of classical liberalism as F. A. Hayek could recognize (Hayek is credited as a founding father of the libertarian branch of liberalism), holding

12. Morgan Phillips, "Merriam-Webster changes its definition of 'sexual preference' as Barrett gets called out for using term," *Fox News*, October 14, 2020.

13. For the postmodern context behind these newly defined terms within the woke vocabulary, see Helen Pluckrose and James Lindsay, *Cynical Theories: How Activist Scholarship Made Everything about Race, Gender, and Identity and Why This Harms Everybody* (Durham, NC: Pitchstone Publishing, 2020).

up the edifice of liberalism was the bedrock belief in the "individual."[14] That was a magical creation. No one outside of the West had ever thought of it. The rise of woke culture has called into question whether it was ever real. Nietzsche anticipated our wavering confidence. "There exists neither 'spirit,' nor reason, nor thinking, nor consciousness, nor soul, nor will, nor truth," as he concluded: "all are fictions that are of no use."[15] Even with the aid of classical philosophy it is difficult for reason to prove the soul immortal. Without the aid of religion such a feat is proving practically impossible. Once upon a time, the "individual" was imbued with dignity, was more than his race, was greater than the sum of his sexual appetites, was free, was responsible, and was, as a practical outworking of such principles, to be treated fairly under the law. The individual was, in short, made in the *imago Dei.* And neither the new left nor what remains of our classical liberals believes it.

Or do they? The next decades will tell. The up-close presence of Islam and the rise of woke culture are together forcing the crisis. Whether the dream of universal equality and freedom will stand up against the reality of these new illiberal contenders is the civilizational question of our moment. What is also to be seen is whether this crisis might not turn some back to Christianity in the search for something more solid. In any case, the trial is upon us. And irrespective of how well we like religion, it was only Christianity as it lived through the fire of the Enlightenment that gave the idea of an individual its definite, legal form. By communicating to us a set of prepolitical convictions about the inherent worth of individuals, it regulated how we would treat each other in public. Religion set up our common signage. Now that we're taking those signs down the streets also have grown unsafe. Given the hyperpluralism of our time, and the public disavowal of Christianity as an implicit guide, such calls for "public reason" will ring more and more hollow as the days pass. Diversity has become our greatest weakness.

14. F.A. Hayek, *The Road to Serfdom*, ed. Bruce Caldwell (Chicago: University of Chicago Press, 2007 [1944]), 67–68.

15. Friedrich Nietzsche, *The Will to Power*, trans. Walter Kaufmann and R.J. Hollingdale (New York: Vintage Books, 1968), bk 3, sect 480.

Returning to our earlier question, yes, religion can move people to violence. But this is practically irrelevant; so can anything else. And these days it is the *absence* of religion that has created a vacuum into which illiberal and aggressive forms of politics have marched, reminiscent, alas, of the 1930s on the continent. When secularists committed to the absolute separation between religion and public life say we must keep the wall for the sake of peace, they are setting a smokescreen. For most centuries Christianity has been deemed essential to maintain peace. "Hitherto, it has been considered," Newman observes, "that religion alone" was strong enough to secure submission to law and order; now, however, philosophers and politicians are "bent on satisfying this problem without the aid of Christianity."[16] Faith needs reason to purify it of superstition. Even more, though, reason needs faith to give it confidence in the objectivity of the moral order. History—especially modern history—largely supports this longstanding judgment. We do well to recall, for instance, that more people were executed in a single month during the anti-Christian French Revolution than during the several-hundred-year history of the Spanish Inquisition.[17] Judged by the results of the spinoff modern revolutions in Mexico, Russia, Spain, and then China, wherever atheism has spread among elites, politics has only gone from bad to worse. It was, after all,

16. See *BS*.

17. Historians now place the number killed by the Spanish Inquisition at somewhere just above 3,000. Edward Peters puts the number of deaths between 1550–1800 at "around 3,000" in his *Inquisition* (Berkeley, CA: University of California Press, 1988), 87. Perhaps the leading world authority on the subject, Henry Kamen, gives a lower estimate of "a maximum of three thousand persons" killed "during the entire history of the tribunal" and says that, according to documentary evidence, about 1.8 percent of those tried by the tribunals were ever killed: *The Spanish Inquisition: A Historical Revision*, 4th ed. (New Haven, CT: Yale University Press, 2014), 253–54. For orientation see also Rodney Stark's *Bearing False Witness: Debunking Centuries of Anti-Catholic History* (Conshohocken, PA: Templeton Press, 2016). By contrast, during December of 1793 alone, revolutionary tribunals of the French Republic executed some 3,500 "enemies of the Republic"; see the entry "Terror" in the *Critical Dictionary of the French Revolution*, ed. F. Furet and Mona Ozouf (Cambridge, MA: The Belknap Press, 1989), 143.

atheistic communist regimes of the twentieth century that were responsible directly for the killing outside of war of some one hundred million citizens.[18]

IV

With the birth of officially secular regimes over the last 200 years, we in the West have found ourselves in the unique historical position of being able to evaluate the gains and losses of secularization. However we weigh the outcomes, even those without faith have begun to admit doubts. Is it possible that trying to imagine a future for Western culture apart from Christianity amounts to saying we won't have a Western culture? Is it possible that the roots of faith go too deep? That if the roots go, the plant will wither? More are beginning to wonder. As the English atheist Don Cupitt has written, "Nobody in the West can be wholly non-Christian. You may call yourself non-Christian, but the dreams you dream are still Christian dreams."[19] The German atheist philosopher Jürgen Habermas also moved closer to this view. For the past half century Habermas served, alongside Rawls, as the leading spokesman for a purely secular politics. In his late work he stressed the need to renew the dialogue with religion. Surveying the recent history of the West he too openly acknowledged that nations without gods seem incapable of inspiring deep loyalty. *Sans* gods, *sans* faith, *sans* liturgy, reason's results disappoint.[20]

For a believer, the rationale is obvious. Technical procedures alone were never intended to float the armada of Democracy. Underneath

18. Figure from Stéphane Courtois and Nicolas Werth, et al., trans. J. Murphy and M. Kramer, *Black Book of Communism: Crimes, Terror, Repression* (Cambridge, MA: Harvard University Press, 1999), 4.

19. Don Cupitt, *The Meaning of the West: An Apology for Secular Christianity* (London: SCM Press, 2008), 67.

20. For Habermas's reflections on this theme, see Jürgen Habermas, et al., *An Awareness of What Is Missing: Faith and Reason in a Post-Secular Age* (London: Polity Press, 2010).

it all were cultural currents that we needed to keep the project moving in a humane direction: the dignity of the person, the fact of solidarity, the trust in progress, the hope of heaven. Habermas went even further. Given the failure of modern reason to extract itself from the pathologies of secular society—its violence, its loneliness, and its doubt—Habermas proposes that secular society has entered a new phase. If we are not simply to despair of reason altogether, as did Nietzsche, secular moderns must move beyond the strategies of the Enlightenment. Religion, despite expectations, is not going away. In many domains, where secular culture has collapsed, religion abides, bringing comfort, insight, and inspiration to clever and simple without distinction. Given these empirical realities, Habermas proposes that nonreligious Westerners must be open again to finding resources for politics within religion. Secular thinkers, he concludes, have "good reasons to be willing to learn from religious traditions."[21]

Does religion breed violence? Perhaps. Or perhaps the way we have been taught to state the question was never helpful. Following Newman, a more interesting question than whether religion causes violence is: Could a godless state ever sustain civility? Newman's distinct contribution to undermining the myth of endless religious violence lies not so much in a correction to our knowledge of historical facts about religion as to a more refined sense of human motivation—and of what kinds of goods deserve public honor. In other words, thinking about political order along lines that Newman prefers gives us grounds at the least to propose that the myth of religious violence may be nothing other than a convenient story. Indeed, when confronted with the historical and present reality of the violence of the godless, secularists often do not necessarily feel their theory threatened. There is a philosophical reason for this. The first myth of modernity was always supported by a second. Religion indeed can contribute to conflicts. But anyone who has reflected on

21. Jürgen Habermas in Habermas and Ratzinger, *The Dialectics of Secularization: On Reason and Religion*, trans. Brian McNeil, C.R.V. (San Francisco: Ignatius Press, 2005), 42.

the history and origin of wars knows that many other objects of love, such as real estate, typically figure within the equation. By removing religion from the realm of public reason, by casting metaphysical claims into the realm of mere speculation, the theory was that men would no longer fight at all. Peace was the early modern promise. Whatever peace we got came at a high cost, perhaps too high a cost. Either way, the early modern strategy could be plausible only *if* religious belief was unhinged from public knowledge.

V

And so we arrive at the second myth: the conflict between reason and faith. Science, in this myth, is grounded in an objective and neutral reason, faith in imagination, sentiment, or will. Reason may not tell us about metaphysics, so the thinking runs, but at least it can help us build bridges and vaccines, and these, unlike the goods of religion, are worthy of our public esteem. Newman's distinctive contribution in this domain, I believe, is to help give us a vision for what an enlarged public reason could look like.

Already by the nineteenth century, philosophers of the Enlightenment had implanted in the Western imagination a persuasive story. It is a story about the goodness of reason, and the unnecessary complications of faith. In his early *University Sermons*, before an audience of professors and students at Oxford, Newman examined directly the relationship between faith and reason. One of the chief difficulties in properly grasping their relation, he says, has to do with correctly defining terms. This is not a bad place for us to begin as well. In general our understanding of each requires revision. Newman finds that in the popular (and mistaken) view, reason demands strong evidence before it assents, whereas faith is content with weak evidence.[22] Focusing on the concept of "reason," Newman identifies three popular but inadequate uses of the word. While each usage contains some element of truth, taken singly or

22. *US* Sermon 10.17.

without qualification, together they distort our notion, and pave the way to a false dichotomy between faith and reason.[23]

One popular sense of reason denotes an "expertise in logical argument."[24] As one would expect, there is some truth to this description. Reason certainly does manifest itself in cogent argument. Strictly, an argument is a series of propositions leading from known premises to a hitherto unknown conclusion. The problem with limiting reason in this way is that the definition is too *narrow*. If facility with the syllogism were reason's only mark, claims that failed to follow demonstratively from evident premises could never be justifiably held. But nobody actually reasons this way. As Newman insists, we correctly hold many beliefs not arrived at through a syllogism. And armed with only the syllogism, how could one ever find trustworthy premises in the first place? If we were to limit reason in this way all intuition would be discounted, as would likely guesses, probable judgments, quick decisions based upon limited facts, as would the educated hunches of doctors, detectives, and lovers considering the leap into that unknown future that is marriage.

Another popular sense of the term denotes a mind that considers nothing but "the actual evidence producible in its favour."[25] This sense of reason is broader, but still too constricting. It would be unreasonable to discount all authority. Again, we may perform a *reductio ad absurdum*. If this were the sum of reason, then the mind should always withhold assent from whatever it did not see directly *for itself*. Your dictum here would be: if you cannot see it you should not believe it. While one certainly should respect the difference between what one sees directly and what one hears from another, the distinction itself does not entail a categorical difference. Both mental states, "seeing" and "hearing," can be expressions of "reason." Should we accept such a definition, learning from teachers

23. In Newman's preface to the 1871 edition of the *University Sermons*, he identifies some fifteen propositions and numerous illustrative quotations from these sermons, which I here follow; see also Thomas J. Norris's helpful review in his essay "Faith" in the *Cambridge Companion to John Henry Newman*, ed. Ian Ker and Terrence Merrigan (Cambridge: Cambridge University Press, 2009), 73–97.

24. *US* preface, xiv.

25. *US* Sermon 10.26.

would cease. Limit reason in this way and peer review would grind to a halt, schools would close, parenting would become impossible. In religion, we would all be forced to become Unitarians. Belief in the Holy Trinity would be absurd since the Church has never claimed to "reason to it," but accepts it on the basis of a very good authority whom it would be most foolish not to trust.

No, learning depends upon docility. To withhold trust at all cost would be a sign of mania. This mistaken view of reason borders on solipsism—the fantasy that nothing exists outside your own head, and Newman was no solipsist. He mentions one final mistaken view: to believe that the human mind is an organ of infinite and unsurpassable power. Since Newman believed in an infinitely wise God, he rejects also this description. Where the first two definitions overly constrict the estimation of our own powers, this last wildly overreaches it.

Newman's aim in these homilies is, of course, not to denigrate reason. His hope is both to enlarge our sense of its scope and soberly to reckon the limits of its power. Reasoning encompasses a far broader array of powers and sources than is commonly allowed. Where a contrast is needed, it would be better to distinguish not reason from faith, but reason from *authority*. Positively, he concludes with a helpful definition. Reasoning is no more and no less than "any process or act of the mind, by which, from knowing one thing it advances on to know another."[26] Faith and reason remain distinct. But they remain acts of the same mind. Faith itself, in this broader view, is likewise "an exercise of reason."[27] Where natural reason begins thinking from principles evident by nature, what we call faith is the same reason illuminated by principles that have been introduced from an authority that speaks from *above* nature.

Returning to our main discussion, Newman rejects the caricature of a conflict. Science and faith *both* engage reason. In another place, Newman makes more vivid how these two pursuits of the mind differ. For one thing, they typically address differing objects. The theologian's God is immaterial whereas the geologist's rock is not. In all

26. Ibid., 12.2.
27. Ibid., 11.9.

disciplines one must keep in working order the appropriate instruments of study. Since the theologian seeks to know a being that is all good, special obligations arise. The instrument of his mind must be cleansed; he too must become like the thing—in this case the person—he wishes to know. He must be *pure of heart.* At the level of intellectual method Newman notes another difference. Where the natural sciences use inductive operations of reason, theology is concerned chiefly with deductive acts. On the side of physics, the method of argumentation begins first from the experience of the senses. "In physics," Newman explains, "a vast and omnigenous mass of information lies before the inquirer, all in a confused litter"; reason's work in this discipline is to arrange and analyze, and then to draw conclusions based upon experiences given. Slowly, and over time, a body of knowledge is built upon and supported by an expanding base of experiential observations. With theology, reason's work proceeds the other way. Instead of beginning with scattered experience, the mind begins with revelation. "What is known in Christianity," he concludes, "is just that which is revealed, and nothing more."[28] As St. Paul says, faith comes "from hearing."[29] Reason starts with words and deeds communicated by God, and only then does theology proper begin its work. The Holy Trinity can only be accepted on the basis of authority, as can the incarnation of Christ, and the real presence in the Eucharist. Other doctrines, of course, such as the existence of God, or the morality of human acts, are conclusions that may be proven either by the witness of the Bible or through reflection upon nature, that is, through deductive or inductive methods.

Whatever else one may say about reason and faith, one thing is clear: the two can never clash. Physics and theology hold different objects, require different methods, and yield different *classes* of conclusions. Whereas physics, biology, and chemistry are interested chiefly in efficient causes (how things work), theologians, like philosophers, want chiefly to know final causes (why things work);

28. *Idea*, "Christianity and Physical Science," sec. 6, 331.
29. Romans 10:17.

whereas natural science is concerned most with the created order, theology is concerned most with the Author of that order. Newman sums up this way: "On the whole, the two studies do most surely occupy distinct fields, in which each may teach without expecting any interposition from the other."[30] Newman has much more to say about the relation between faith and reason, but for us who would enter into a complex dialogue with unbelievers about the public status of knowledge or the relation between science and religion, he would bid us believe the two compatible, and encourage us to understand why they could never, in principle, conflict.

VI

So much for Newman's basic framework; let's consider next some of our own more common objections. Those committed to the "clash" narrative typically appeal to three families of counterarguments: one based on psychology, another based on sociology, and a third based on the success of the scientific method.

The first we'll name the *psychological* objection, logically the weakest though perhaps the most widely held position. The secularist might concede with Newman that physical science tells us nothing about final purposes, nothing about the afterlife. Men and women, a secularist would point out, are looking for pleasures beyond what their present circumstances can deliver. Believers seek religion as a "consolation." Is it not then a psychological *motive*, a mere desire for comfort—and not a rational cause—that leads most to accept revelation? When this sort of objection is raised, note what is and is not being affirmed. The objector here may see religion as something good for people; it may be useful or necessary to personal or social happiness. The only problem is that its claims are not true. Religion, says Marx, "is the sigh of the oppressed creature"; it is "the heart of a heartless world and the soul of soulless conditions. It is the opium of the people." Or as Sigmund Freud put it, religion

30. *Idea*, 2.7.5, "Christianity and Physical Science," 330.

is the "illusion" that "derives its strength from its readiness to fit in with our instinctual wishful impulses."[31]

On logical grounds the psychological objection to faith is weak. More precisely, the objection is irrelevant. Whether a theory makes me happy or not communicates nothing about the truth or falsity of its claim; explaining motives does not disprove conclusions. It may happen to be more convenient to believe that this rattle snake won't actually kill me; but whether or not my heart stops after its bite has nothing to do with my *wishes*. Even more, the premise upon which this nineteenth century doubt is based has grown dubious. For much of the world today the connection between religion and personal happiness has grown weaker. At the hands of atheistic regimes, the twentieth century saw more Christians martyred than all other centuries combined. In the twenty-first century Christians continue to be the group that suffers by far the most widespread persecution, typically at the hands of Moslems. Some 260 million believers, or about one in nine Christians now suffer "high levels" of persecution according to the *World Watch List*. What this translates into in a single year is some 3,000 Christians killed for their faith, some 4,000 imprisoned for their faith, and some ten thousand churches or buildings owned by Christian groups attacked on account of their faith.[32] And, even in North America, to represent Christian views in public means you are likely to find your career in jeopardy and your reputation subject to slander.

But let's set this experience of the last one hundred years aside. Against the fact of persecutions, we can grant that faith *does* offer a sort of pleasure and often does make people by some description "happy." How might this be considered evidence against religion?

31. Karl Marx, *Critique of Hegel's Philosophy of Right*, ed. Joseph O'Malley (Cambridge: University of Cambridge Press, 1970), 131; Sigmund Freud, "A Philosophy of Life (The Question of a Weltanschauung)" in *New Introductory Lectures on Psycho-analysis*, vol 22, lecture 35, trans. and ed. by James Strachey (London: Hogarth Press, 1973), 175.

32. These according to the *World Watch List*, an annual publication sponsored by the *Open Doors Organization* tracking persecution in the fifty most dangerous countries for Christians to live in. For a summary of statistics see: www.opendoorsusa.org/christian-persecution/world-watch-list.

We certainly can concede that the mind has a generous capacity for self-delusion. A cursory view of the contents of the DSM-5 (the *Diagnostic and Statistical Manual of Mental Disorders*) is evidence enough of the range of maladies that can inflict our perceptions. In theological terms, the proclivity to miss the mark has a name: original sin. Yet sickness is a parody of health. And a *dis*order witnesses always to some more fundamental order, some more basic reality that has been mangled. The attraction of pleasure that both madmen and sinners feel does not teach us that pleasure is bad. It teaches us that humans can seek good things in the wrong places. Evil is a *corruptio boni*, a corruption of the good.

Even more, in most domains we rightly take our pleasures to offer a rough guide to truth. Consider a thought experiment. Your stomach is in knots and your breathing is short. You visit your doctor. He questions you. You tell him that you have eliminated meat and taken up smoking pot. He is likely to propose that you change your habits and then return in a month. Suppose that over this month you drop the tofu, get back to the Alberta beef, and quit smoking altogether. You begin to feel better, and you tell your doctor so. What should the doctor conclude? Probably that steaks are good for you and that dope is bad. Similarly, when our expectations in empirical science, in love, or in economics "fit" with reality, when they lead to the results we anticipate, we tend to take this as evidence for their truth. Should religion be treated as a special case? I see no reason for that. Christianity does claim, in a manner, to make us happy both in this life and the next. When believers testify that the medicine works, that does not offer a full demonstration—placebos sometimes produce good effects too; but it is at least the sort of evidence that would normally inspire further investigation.

Another objection is rooted in the sociology of science. I refer here to what we might call an appeal to the authority and prestige of unbelieving scientists. This sort of objection runs as follows: as more people gained access to scientific training they too would adopt a scientific outlook and forsake their religious doctrine. The claim here seems to be that *real* scientists know that faith can never be reconciled to reason. Religion may persist for a time, but its time will come. As science and democracy advance, religion will fade.

This is the intuition behind the so-called "secularization" thesis that held sway among sociologists like Max Weber (1864–1920), and philosophers like John Dewey (1859–1952), up till the present.

While it is true that religious practice in the West has declined, the relationship between modernity and religiosity is by no means one of asymmetry. Despite the ubiquity of cell phones, the internet, and globalized markets, religion has not vanished. This reality is more commonly acknowledged in the West since the terrorist attacks of 9/11, after which there was a temporary revival of church attendance and a more generalized disparaging of a purely materialistic ethic. But for years before that, evidence for the secularization thesis was already disappearing. As the noted sociologist Peter Berger put it in the 1990s, "the assumption we live in a secularized world is false." Our world, he concluded, "is as furiously religious as ever."[33] In some places and times and among some groups, also today, higher education is correlated to higher levels of religious belief.[34] Indeed, even committed secularists recognize that the persistence of religious belief, also in the West, remains a difficult fact for their theory to overcome. "The universal propensity toward religious beliefs," evolutionary psychologist and atheist Steven Pinker muses "is a genuine scientific puzzle."[35] I partially agree. The bigger question though, it seems to me, is why some scientists insist on trying to wish away the phenomenon they purport to study. Perhaps the puzzle is: why are secularists so dogmatic about a godless future? By pinning hopes on an ever-receding tomorrow, by trading on the testimony of high-profile atheists, the secularization thesis can never be falsified by the facts of the present. Such is normally the mark of an unhelpful theory.

33. Peter Berger, *The Desecularization of the World: Resurgent Religion and World Politics* (Grand Rapids: William B. Eerdmans, 1999), 2.

34. Some of the evidence is reviewed in Mary Eberstadt's *How the West Really Lost God*, 214.

35. Steven Pinker, "The Evolutionary Psychology of Religion," *Freethought Today*, 22:1 (January–February 2005), presented at the *Annual Meeting of the Freedom from Religion Foundation*, Madison, WI, October 29, 2004, at www.ffrf.org/about/getting-acquainted/item/13184-the-evolutionary-psychology-of-religion.

But is it the case that most, or even "the best" scientists, believe in a naturalistic view of the universe? The history of science does not strongly support this presumption. When glancing at the history of scientific discovery, what one notices is that scores of founding scientists in fields of empirical research were not only theists but active members of the clergy. Cherry-picking across the centuries one could include Cardinal Nicholas of Cusa (d. 1446), possibly the first to have discovered the treatment of myopia (shortsightedness), Blessed Nicholas Stenu (d. 1686), one of the founders of modern geology, Gregory Mendel (d. 1884), a Benedictine monk and originator of the modern study of genetics, and Georges Lemaitre (d. 1966), founder of the Big Bang theory in modern astrophysics. If one were to include believing Protestant and Catholic laymen who were founding scientists, that list would of course be greatly expanded.[36]

If the past gives little basis for the belief that scientific training excludes religious devotion, neither does the present. When Steven Pinker tells us that religion's persistence is "a puzzle" we should not regard him as a representative of the larger scientific community. When contemporary scientists are asked this question, only a minority think religion and science in some sense fundamentally conflict. Among US scientists, for example, more scientists now believe in God than do not. In some countries, if you are a scientist, you are even likely to be more *devout* a believer than is the average non-scientist.[37]

If the first two objections relate to the psychology of religion and the sociology of scientists, the final one focuses on the undisputed

36. For references, see Topping, *The Gift of the Church* (Charlotte, NC: TAN Books, 2018), 68–71.

37. In the United States, 44 percent of scientists believe in God or a higher power whereas 41 percent think no God exists. See the Pew Study "Scientists and Belief" (November 5, 2009), www.pewforum.org/2009/11/05/scientists-and-belief. In some countries—for example, in India, Hong Kong, and Taiwan—more than 50 percent of scientists believe in God, and are more likely to attend weekly services than non-scientists: see Ecklund, Johnson, et al., "Religion Among Scientists in International Context: A New Study of Scientists in Eight Regions," *Socius: Sociological Research for a Dynamic World* (September 2016), figures 1 and 2 and table 3.

explanatory power of the empirical methods. Is there something about the scientific method itself that renders other modes of knowledge redundant or unnecessary?

To answer this question thoroughly would require a lengthy discussion; here I wish to make only a few observations. Newman wrote at a time when the narrative of the "conflict between religions and science" was newly in the air. This or something close to it was an objection that was put to him directly by a friend. Newman was a contemporary of Charles Darwin (1809–1882) and when he was asked to offer a defense of religion in the face of advancing scientific discoveries, Newman conceded that the religious believer had reason to pause. He admitted that the "enlargement of the circle of secular knowledge" certainly can have the effect of making many consider that its limit will be without end.[38] He agreed that the advances of the natural sciences *could* encourage moral and religious scepticism. Particularly when someone less educated in the philosophical foundations of their faith confronts a scientific claim—for example, that the first human may have evolved from apes—such a faith might feel unsure. To these his first counsel was to *patience*. What appears to be a truth of science in one decade is often overthrown in another.[39]

Besides suggesting patience, Newman offered a clarification. When others insisted that science should lead to a decrease of faith, Newman's answer was one of bemusement. It was not clear what *about* science, precisely, conflicted with Catholic faith. One of the greatest problems one has in defending the faith for such people, he said, is that "it is so difficult to say precisely what it is that is to be encountered and overthrown."[40] When doubts plague, the contemporary Catholic should arm himself with historical precedent, he said. The long history of the relation between the Catholic Church and Western science is, mostly, the story of a love affair. It was the Catholic Church that early promoted and sustained education in

38. *Apo* v, 260.

39. An example from Newman's time is the theory of "spontaneous generation," disproved as it happens by the chemist (and devout Catholic) Louis Pasteur.

40. *Apo* v, 262.

the West through catechetical and monastic schools. It is the Catholic Church that has taken an abiding interest in educating the poor. It is the Catholic Church that founded and built Europe's university system.[41] And for those who cite the Church's conflict with Galileo as an instance of the Church's distrust of free enquiry, Newman's reply is laconic: *exceptio probat regulam*. The exception proves the rule, for the Galileo case "is the one stalk argument" trotted out because there is not a second to be found.[42]

That is overstating the case. The other commonly cited evidence for a clash is the theory of evolution. In 1868, about a decade after Darwin published *On the Origins of Species*, a fellow priest pressed Newman to consider the theory. Newman was clear that he was not in a position to judge the merit of Darwin's observations and conclusions, from a scientific view. But, if Darwin's theory were found to be true, Newman thought that it should prove no difficulty whatsoever to Christians. "It does not seem to me to follow that creation is denied," Newman counselled, "because the Creator, millions of years ago, gave laws to matter. He first created matter and then he created laws for it—laws which should *construct* it into its present wonderful beauty, and accurate adjustment and harmony of parts *gradually*." He goes on to clarify:

> If Mr Darwin in this or that point of his theory comes into collision with revealed truth, that is another matter—but I do not see that the principle of development, or what I have called construction, does. As to the Divine Design, is it not an instance of incomprehensibly and infinitely marvellous Wisdom and Design to have given certain laws to matter millions of ages ago, which have surely and precisely worked out, in the long course of those ages, those effects which He from the first proposed.[43]

In our time, many scientists have internalized Newman's insight and accepted the distinction between primary and secondary causation (well defended of course already by the medieval scholastics). In short: your method always has to be suited to the object you are

41. For orientation to the scholarship, see Topping, *Gift of the Church*, 68–80.
42. *Apo* v, 264.
43. *LD* xxiv, 77–78.

looking to know about. If you want to know about non-physical things, you must look for non-material methods of knowing (as for example, in mathematics). The renowned physicist and one-time leader of the Human Genome Project, Francis Collins, for instance, relates a parable to illustrate how narrow is the new atheists' view of knowledge. He tells of a man who decided to study deep-sea life using a net whose mesh was three inches wide. "After catching many wild and wonderful creatures from the depths, the man concluded that there are no deep-sea fish that are smaller than three inches in length!"[44] The point: to catch the fish you are looking for, you need the right sort of net; since God is not material, you cannot search for him under microscopes and telescopes. The divine creator bequeaths being to creatures and preserves the laws that govern their interactions; the natural scientist explores those laws and attempts to express their universal character. The overwhelming testimony of philosophers and scientists, past and present, gives good reason to think there is ample room for both an immaterial God and for material methods of enquiry.

I have made no attempt to describe the nature and scope of those other types of methods for gaining knowledge that exist beyond the scientific method. My aim here has been more modest. In looking to Newman's distinctions, and in considering a few of the more common objections of our contemporaries, I have only tried to offer plausible reasons to think faith and reason need not conflict. When evangelizing, we need constantly to undermine the myths that only religion causes conflict and that only science uncovers truth. The third myth, that dignity requires autonomy, is supported by a distinctive late-modern view of conscience, which we take up next.

44. Francis Collins, *The Language of God: A Scientist Presents Evidence for Belief* (New York: Free Press, 2006), 229.

7

Anchoring Conscience

"Our great internal teacher of religion is… Conscience"[1]

I

An unintended consequence of the Second Vatican Council was that the notion of conscience came to be deployed so as to undermine the Church's authority. The confusion unleashed by the Council is partially understandable. Vatican II proclaimed both a greater reverence for the rights of individuals, as well as a deeper awareness of the responsibility of the laity. At a high point in the Council's rhetoric, conscience is described, for one, as "the most secret core and sanctuary of man." In this place man is "alone with God," whose voice "echoes in his depths."[2] Conscience here seems to grant the individual access to moral truth unmediated by political or ecclesial structures. Conscience is a sanctuary. Does this mean its dictates are divine?

To this serene praise is joined an invigorating call to lay responsibility. "Let the laity," the Council fathers implored, "by their combined efforts remedy any institutions and conditions of the world which are customarily an inducement to sin." To this end, the Council attempted to curb what it deemed an excessive dependence upon clerical judgments on secular questions; it called upon the baptized not to "imagine that his pastors are always such experts," or that to every problem clergy "can readily give him a concrete

1. *GA* part 2, ch. 10, 389.
2. *Gaudium et Spes*, 16.

solution, or even that such is their mission."[3] A reasonable precept. Priests may or may not be experts on penicillin. Bishops may or may not have clever proposals for tax reform. But contexts matter. Individual statements and even major themes within the Council were often interpreted as though they could be read apart from their textual setting and abstracted from the broader doctrinal tradition from which those texts emerged. The Council's teaching on conscience, for one, which affirms the link between human interiority and divine justice, came by some to be interpreted not through the lens of holy tradition but rather by the flickering lights of Kant, Rousseau, and Nietzsche.

The third grand myth of modernity is that dignity demands radical autonomy. One privileged expression of autonomy is in the exercise of conscience. Where we moderns tend to view conscience as an unassailable oracle, Newman calls conscience an organ for perceiving moral truth; where a majority of Catholics today think conscience frees us from authority, for Newman the voice of conscience points to a future judgment. Rediscovering Newman's teaching on how to anchor conscience in the objective sources of morality is, surely, one of the most effective means for unseating this final myth.

II

At the origins of secular modernity emerged the claim that human freedom requires autonomy. Immanuel Kant (1724–1804), here in this precept as with so many others, is the faithful spokesperson for the project. "Dare to be free!" was the taunt of the philosopher. To be free is above all to be autonomous. Autonomy means literally to act as "a law unto oneself" (from the Greek: *auto*, self; *nomos*, law). Each man is supposed to be a self-appointed judge of his own conduct. To act with autonomy is to accept the full responsibility of freedom. By contrast, those who look for external guidance, to the family, to the state, above all to religion, remain stunted in their

3. Ibid., 36 and 43.

humanity. To function as a *dependent* rational animal is in Kant's terminology to act according to *heteronomy*, the rule of others (*heteros*, other; *nomos*, law).[4] Although Kant recognized the necessity of an objective moral law, and that God must exist if our moral intuitions are to be other than absurd, the creator and the moral order are not for him matters of knowledge, strictly speaking. Conscience is the site merely where reason deliberates within itself about action. And it is a court which admits no advisors, not even the Almighty.[5]

The other counterpoint of the Enlightenment era, Rousseau (1712–1778), will arrive at a similar conclusion, though laying greater stress on the interiority of the act. Conscience, likewise, reigns supreme for Rousseau. Its autonomous exercise expresses our *authentic* freedom, a freedom unspoiled by the acid rain of social convention. In a telling passage, found within Rousseau's masterpiece on education, he declares the authentic, natural man's break from an objectively ordered conscience:

> Conscience, conscience! Divine instinct, immortal and celestial voice, certain guide of a being that is ignorant and limited but intelligent and free; infallible judge of good and bad which makes man like unto God; it is you who make the excellence of his nature and the morality of his actions. Without you I sense nothing in me that raises me above the beasts, other than the sad privilege of leading myself astray from error to error with the aid of an understanding without rule and a reason without principle.[6]

Conscience separates man from beasts; it guides ignorant creatures in their judgements of good and evil; and it makes man like unto God. Except note this difference: the link between the natural man's

4. Kant's manifesto *What Is Enlightenment* (1784) is found in the collection of Kant's work translated by Mary J. Gregor, *Practical Philosophy* (Cambridge: Cambridge University Press, 1996), 11–22.

5. So constricted is Kant's view of reason that not even if God should come to earth would he allow that one could teach another through example. "Even the Holy One of the Gospel must first be compared with our ideal of moral perfection before he is cognized as such": *Groundwork of the Metaphysics of Morals*, trans. and ed. Mary Gregor (Cambridge: Cambridge University Press, 1997), 21.

6. Rousseau, *Emile: Or On Education*, trans. Allan Bloom (New York: Basic Books, 1979), Bk 4, 290.

conscience and prudence is now severed from every social or ecclesial norm. Without revelation, without tradition, without the Holy Spirit, fallible man has been thrown back upon a private, intensely interior, "infallible judge." Though both Kant and Rousseau see some remote position for God within their moral theories, their intellectual heirs will not.

When the German Augustinian monk Martin Luther defied the Church at the Diet of Worms in 1521 with his "Here I stand, I can do no other" declaration, he could not have foreseen the train of consequences that were to follow. But follow they did. In the initial phases of modernity, unleashed with the Protestant Reformation, the individual's conscience was liberated from the tyranny of institutions claiming to speak for God; in its last phase, conscience wars against God Himself. Over the course of the nineteenth and twentieth centuries, Friedrich Nietzsche (1844–1900), his intellectual cousins, and his legion of disciples asked a set of uncomfortable but logical questions about the status of our moral knowledge. If God is indeed dead, or at least unknowable by reason, what regard should we show for religious codes and systems of ethics? Indeed, if law opposes the autonomy of conscience, shouldn't conscience fight back to oppose the tyranny of law? If law no longer expresses reason, but is merely an external force, wouldn't the noble rise up against its oppression?

The growing consensus of recent years has been: yes. If God is dead, all is in principle permissible. Religion, parents, government, law, the police, are all the enemies of freedom so understood. The worldly wise see it and the unscrupulously courageous live it. Overcoming convention takes on a heroic quality. Rebellion and professional activism becomes romantic, perhaps even a matter for state subsidies. As one of Dostoevsky's (1821–1881) characters put it, within the new moral order "it's now considered a man's right, if he wants something very much, not to stop at any obstacle, even if he has to do in eight persons to that end."[7] Guilt and shame are prejudices to overcome, the debris left on the side of the mountain of our

7. Lebedev in Dostoevsky's *The Idiot*, trans. R. Pevear and L. Volokhonsky (Toronto: Alfred A. Knopf, 2002), part 2.7, 257.

human nature that needs to be clear-cut of alien growth. Beneath the untidy vegetation and lumbering pines of the conscience lies nothing but the bare rock of will. And it is a will *to power.* The concept of "bad guilt" must be understood against the violence of this new scene playing out upon our culture. Bad guilt is a sign of weakness. It describes the *consciousness* of one whose mind has been stripped bare of the constraints of so-called good and evil, but for all of that, still feels the *pain of conscience.* Nietzsche's account is precise. "Hostility, cruelty, joy in persecuting, in attacking, in change, in destruction—all this turned against the possessors of such instincts: that is the origin of the 'bad conscience.'"[8] Newman too saw how the logic would unfold. Conscience, he said, now designates "the right of thinking, speaking, writing, acting, according to one's judgment or . . . humour, without any thought of God at all." Secular conscience is little more than, he says, "the right of self-will."[9]

Today, divine law and human freedom engage in trench warfare. Any concession for one side is reckoned a loss for the other. As Jean-Paul Sartre (1905–1980) put it, "man is a being whose existence precedes his essence."[10] We have no nature, no form, no purpose. We make of ourselves whatever we would become. Freedom is absolute. As a matter of principle, the concept of a Creator must collide against such a vision of a creature. We can put this popular atheistic view syllogistically: if God exists, I cannot be free; but I am free; *therefore God does not exist.* Deny God and it becomes difficult to affirm a specific purpose for freedom. Even here in North America, the effect of bad metaphysics has made itself felt at the level of public policy. When the choice comes to deference to God or an emancipated conscience, our public institutions have of late become unequivocal. In the infamous words of the US Chief Justice Anthony Kennedy: if freedom is to mean anything, if autonomy, if conscience, if dignity are to remain intact, then human freedom

8. Nietzsche, *On the Genealogy of Morals*, trans W. Kaufmann and R.J. Hollingdale (New York: Vintage Books, 1989), section 85.

9. *LDN* 5.250.

10. See his manifesto "Existentialism is a Humanism," in *Existentialism from Dostoyevsky to Sartre*, ed. W. Kaufman (New York: Meridian Publishing Company, 1989).

must of itself entail the right "to define one's own concept of existence, of meaning, of the universe and of the mystery of life." For the past fifty years such mystical reasoning has found in our legal apparatus rights to anything from aborting when we wish, to marrying whom we fancy, even to killing ourselves if we must.[11]

III

So much for the children of this age. The myth of autonomy has proven irresistible among Catholics too. Neither ignorance nor infidelity is novel. What is new is the notion that one can persistently and publicly dissent from established teaching and still remain, in one's own estimation, a "good" Catholic. Immediately after the Council, some moral theologians developed the notion of loyal dissent. Half a century later, in North America and in parts of Europe, believers have come widely to accept the claim that one can deny doctrine without separating oneself from communion. To take just a few measures, about one out of three U.S. Catholics say you can be a good Catholic and not believe in Jesus's resurrection (34 percent); about the same number deny the real presence of Christ in the Eucharist (37 percent); 78 percent say you can use artificial contraception, the same number that say you can remain in good standing even if you do not attend Mass every week. Almost nine out of ten

11. In more fulsome words: "These matters, involving the most intimate and personal choices a person may make in a lifetime, choices central to personal dignity and autonomy, are central to the liberty protected by the Fourteenth Amendment. At the heart of liberty is the right to define one's own concept of existence, of meaning, of the universe, and of the mystery of human life" (*Planned Parenthood of Southeastern Pa.* v. *Casey*, 1992); and then again, on gay marriage, from Kennedy's opening line: "The Constitution promises liberty to all within its reach, a liberty that includes certain specific rights that allow persons, within a lawful realm, to define and express their identity" (*Obergefell et. al.* v. *Hodges, Director, Ohio Department of Health, et. al.*, 2015); on a supposed right to kill oneself, it took the Canadian Supreme Court until recently to discover it implied in the Charter's section 7 protection of the right to "life, liberty, and the security of the person," in *Carter v. Canada* 2015 SCC 5, paras 70 and 126. Though, wonderfully, how far *Dobbs* v. *Jackson* (2022) will go toward undoing some of this damage in our legal culture, now that *Roe* v. *Wade* has been undone, is to be seen.

(86 percent) assert that you can disagree with Church teaching and still remain, yes, "loyal to the Church."[12] It is no wonder that believers feel the ark of the Church is heaving. Navigating Catholic identity has become like sailing in a fog. From a psychological point of view, what has made possible or at least plausible this union of epistemic denial and sociological self-affirmation is the prior commitment to what has been termed "interpretive autonomy."[13] This is all another way of saying that Catholics have become Kantians. Conscience has become a rule unto itself.

To erroneously define conscience is one thing, to impute innovations to doctrine is another. Irrespective of how a secular person might wish to define conscience, the Council of itself did not baptize interpretative autonomy. From the same Vatican II document we read that through conscience man detects "a law which he does not impose upon himself." Natural law, according to St. Thomas, is and is not an imposition from above. Ratios originate outside of music, yet the third, the interval between *doh* and *mi*, very much resides *within* the musical scale. So also the natural law. Conscience detects principles within itself which *at the same time* originate from outside itself. Reason participates in the natural law, bears witness to the law, applies the law, though it does not invent the law. The Council put it this way: in the formation of conscience, a Christian has the duty "to attend to the sacred and certain doctrine of the Church" and, further, that the Church has the vocation to "confirm by her authority those principles of the moral order"[14] to which conscience must attend—a duty whose contemporary articulation owes much to Cardinal Newman.

In truth, interpretative autonomy has no basis among believers. The Council's energetic call to lay responsibility derives not from Kant or Rousseau but rather from Newman's rally for an educated laity; from his call for a Church filled with men and women steeped

12. For studies, see D'Antonio et al., *Catholics in Transition* (Lanham, MD: Rowman and Littlefield, 2013), 48–60.

13. A term I take from Michele Dillon in *Postsecular Catholicism: Relevance and Renewal* (Oxford: Oxford University Press, 2018), 20.

14. *Dignitatis Humanae*, 14.

in Catholic traditions, capable of uniting reason to the demands of faith, and of exercising an integrating habit of mind:

> I want a laity, not arrogant, not rash in speech, not disputatious, but men who know their religion, who enter into it, who know just where they stand, who know what they hold, and what they do not, who know their creed so well, that they can give an account of it, who know so much of history that they can defend it. I want an intelligent, well-instructed laity; I am not denying you are such already: but I mean to be severe, and, as some would say, exorbitant in my demands, I wish you to enlarge your knowledge, to cultivate your reason, to get an insight into the relation of truth to truth, to learn to view things as they are, to understand how faith and reason stand to each other, what are the bases and principles of Catholicism, and where lie the main inconsistencies and absurdities of the Protestant theory.[15]

This passage bears closer scrutiny. Being "intelligent" here is not equivalent to being "independent" or "willful." The laity that Newman envisions is neither aspirationally progressive nor passively traditional. Rather, it is a laity steeped in the reasons supporting the Creed. In Newman's vision, the laity will learn not merely to parrot teachings once received, but rather to internalize their principles, and then to further them within their own proper sphere of work. Surely, a few laity might excel in the study of academic theology. More directly, Newman is calling the laity to sanctify the secular sphere—the shop, the classroom, the legislature, the home. And during the twentieth century his call found a ready echo in small but mighty movements of the Spirit.

One could show how this call for a theologically educated laity was developed in other documents issued during and after the Council.[16] Perhaps it is more helpful to see how this summons has been embodied in the efforts of groups and individuals. As for the new movements, the spirituality of Opus Dei expresses this theme,

15. *LPC* lecture 9, "Duties of Catholics Towards the Protestant View," 391.

16. See *Apostolicam Actuositatem, On the Apostolate of Lay People* (1965), where the Council calls upon laity to receive a "solid grounding in doctrine . . . in theology, ethics and philosophy" para 29, or John Paul II's 1988 Apostolic Exhortation *Christifideles Laici*, which makes a similar call at paras 59–62.

as does Communion and Liberation and Marriage Encounter. In politics, one could look to the labors of the German Chancellor, Konrad Adenauer (1876–1967), who helped rebuild postwar Europe inspired by principles of Catholic Social Teaching. In the medical sciences, one could point to the work of the Australian physician John Billings (1918–2007) who in the mid-twentieth-century faithfully internalized magisterial teaching on the dignified purposes of sex, and then fructified his own field of study (on human reproductive cycles) in the light of that faith. In education, one might look to the American professor Don Briel (1947–2018) and the "Catholic Studies" movement on North American campuses that he initiated in response to John Paul II's call to relaunch Catholic intellectual life. Those encouraged by these movements, among others, will find in Newman wise inspiration. Newman's call is to cultivate a *faithful reason*, one imbued with the light of faith directed to the sanctification of the secular. It is a call to learn to think in every sphere of human endeavour as though God exists.

IV

If conscience isn't shorthand for radical autonomy, what is it? Newman's positive account of conscience can add clarity. Most importantly, for Newman, conscience is subjective but not relative. It is subjective in that it is our personal link to the divine law reverberating within us; it is objective insofar as it points to a rule, a law, a moral order, that stands in solid shapes beyond the shadows of our own projected wishes. Looking beyond self-appointed dissenters or those who would draw more from secular opinion than from Catholic tradition, the *Catechism* links beautifully the Council with the Cardinal. Conscience, as the *Catechism* clarifies, "is a judgment of reason." The specifically human quality of this act is that we perform it in the light of varied and often morally complicated intentions, objects, and circumstances. The *Catechism* then cites Newman's famous *Letter to the Duke of Norfolk*:

> Conscience is a law of the mind; yet [Christians] would not grant that it is nothing more; I mean that it was not a dictate nor conveyed

> the notion of responsibility, of duty, of a threat and a promise.... [Conscience] is a messenger of him, who, both in nature and in grace, speaks to us behind a veil, and teaches and rules us by his representatives. Conscience is the aboriginal Vicar of Christ.[17]

Conscience is a personal judgment relating law to concrete circumstances. It is also a judgment which can be made more or less well. Contrary to that popular wisdom that would bid us withhold judgment ("Who am I to judge?"), judgment is an essential operation of human reason. Rendering such moral decisions is inevitable; we will be judged for how well we judge.

This aspect of conscience is illuminated well within one of Newman's novels, *Callista: A Tale of the Third Century.* Far into Callista's conversion—a young woman whom we will describe later as an image of a secular, postreligious seeker—she comes to recognize an authority of which she cannot rid herself. At one point along her path to conversion Callista attempts to explain the interior experience of this unseen presence, and the love which draws her to it.

> "Well," she said, "I feel that God within my heart. I feel myself in His presence. He says to me, 'Do this: don't do that.' You may tell me that this dictate is a mere law of my nature, as is to joy or to grieve. I cannot understand this. No, it is the echo of a person speaking to me. Nothing shall persuade me that it does not ultimately proceed from a person external to me. It carries with it its proof of its divine origin. My nature feels towards it as towards a person. When I obey it, I feel a satisfaction; when I disobey, a soreness—just like that which I feel in pleasing or offending some revered friend. So you see, Polemo, I believe in what is more than a mere 'something.' I believe in what is more real to me than sun, moon, stars, and the fair earth, and the voice of friends. You will say, Who is He? Has He ever told you anything about Himself? Alas! no!—the more's the pity! But I will not give up what I have, because I have not more. An echo implies a voice; a voice a speaker. That speaker I love and I fear."[18]

17. CCC 1778.
18. *Cal* chapter 28, 314–15.

Conscience can always err, but it is an error to suppose that conscience can simply be ignored. One may be mistaken about what is good or evil in a given situation; one may mishear the voice of God; but what one can never suppose is that conscience has no claim upon us. Judgment needs to be made.

We should pause over this claim. Conscience provides an echo. It is an instinct for listening to an outside voice. Self-knowledge opens a door to this divine judgment. The *fact* of conscience Newman never doubts. Indeed, elsewhere, this experience of honor and shame, of the sense of an external standard for our conduct, of the praiseworthiness and blameworthiness of some actions, takes on the character of a psychological axiom. His use of the experience of conscience figures prominently, for instance, in one of his proofs for the existence of God. Where Callista offers a moving image of conscience's beckoning voice in the terms of a novel, in *The Grammar of Assent* Newman steps methodically from premises to conclusion.

> As then we have our initial knowledge of the universe through sense, so do we in the first instance begin to learn about its Lord and God from conscience; and, as from particular acts of that instinct, which makes experiences, mere images (as they ultimately are) upon the retina, the means of our perceiving something real beyond them, we go on to draw the general conclusion that there is a vast external world, so from the recurring instances in which conscience acts, forcing upon us importunately the mandate of a Superior, we have fresh and fresh evidence of the existence of a Sovereign Ruler, from whom those particular dictates which we experience proceed; so that, with limitations which cannot here be made without digressing from my main subject, we may, by means of that induction from particular experiences of conscience, have as good a warrant for concluding the Ubiquitous Presence of One Supreme Master, as we have, from parallel experience of sense, for assenting to the fact of a multiform and vast world, material and mental. . . .[19]

An echo implies a voice; a voice a speaker. Accept that the psychological states of honor and shame are rooted in human nature, not

19. *GA* part 1, ch. 4, sec. 1, 63.

merely an accretion of artificial culture, and one has traveled halfway to accepting that nature points to a mind, thus to a law, and therefore to a lawgiver. The experience of conscience offers, he thinks, the "first instance" of God. To explain his argument, Newman draws an analogy. Just as the images that press upon our senses lead us to the conviction that there is a "vast external world" beyond them, so also do the impressions, those "recurring instances" of conscience—of guilt and shame and honor and purity, of the sense of judgment and praise—indicate some Sovereign Ruler. From the sense of obligation, he thinks we can infer the existence of a Judge. Newman's treatment of conscience, in both his imaginative work and his philosophical essay, offers an illustration of how one can take a *longer* approach to apologetics than we are often accustomed. Where Thomas begins arguments for God with the cosmos, Newman prefers to start with the problems encountered by the psyche.[20]

The secular myth of autonomy remains a compelling and consoling story to many. The dream of a limitless freedom measured by the conquest of the body animates the lives of those consumed by a consuming culture. But it is less clear how this fairy tale could ever end well. The environmental, demographic, economic, and moral failures of modernity have exacted a high cost. A pressing task of the Church in the twenty-first century will therefore be to highlight the failures of a social order constructed apart from the Lordship of Jesus Christ. This will be no small undertaking. Given the dominance of secularizing modes of education over the last forty years, such a work will require the effort of two generations, and a willingness to consider afresh the strengths of both old and new models of apologetics.

20. Newman does not disparage the traditional cosmological proofs for God, though he does think they have less appeal. See his nuanced discussion of the place and limit of traditional proofs for God in *Idea*, 2.9–10, "Christianity and Physical Science."

8

Another Kind of Apologetics

"Pray for me, O my friends"[1]

I

What kind of arguments are likely to move today's "nones"? Fulton Sheen (1895–1979), among the Church's most successful evangelists, anticipated the question. Our contemporaries, he observed, are inclined to dismiss reason's positive role in religion. Reason, for moderns, is a tool, an aid to technology, a servant to passions. Classical proofs for God are, therefore, less immediately convincing. The classical approach, developed by Aristotle and St. Thomas, begins from the order of the cosmos and ends at the knowledge of the Creator. While Sheen was a student of this approach, he mastered another. In his televised and popular conferences, he showed, much the way Bishop Robert Barron has for our generation, how Christian wisdom brings light to our questions about education, ethics, and art. No part of culture escapes this integrating vision. If Sheen were alive today, he would think it worth exploring why, for instance, our old are in love with cats and dogs, and why our young are painting themselves with tattoos. In any case, Sheen called this movement of theological reflection from man to God the "anthropological approach."

This approach starts not with the order of the universe but rather with "the disorder inside of man himself." As the bishop explained, by this method we will take all the findings of our psychological age "and use them as a springboard for the presentation of Divine

1. *VV* "Dream of Gerontius," 324.

Truths."[2] It is not that classical and contemporary modes of apologetics conflict in their conclusions. Nor could we ever simply ignore the Church's traditional proofs in favor of God, the soul, and the natural law. It's only that the older method assumes a sort of education now largely absent. In the century before Barron, before Sheen, and before the loss of the liberal arts and a reasonably unified Christian culture, Cardinal Newman had already become a master of this other kind of apologetics. Our own efforts will be enriched by observing some of his principles.

Unlike most professional academics, from a relatively young age, Newman was actively engaged in pastoral work. Newman's service as an Oxford tutor, then an Anglican pastor working amidst both professors and barely literate parishioners, provided him with a wide exposure to the range of personalities and problems that washed over the nineteenth century. This was the century of industry, of the rise of applied science, of globalization, of a yawning gulf between the super-rich and the working class, and of the clash between materialism and Christianity as the two public philosophies vying for the soul of the West. Newman was a good student. His wide exposure to these trends and his parish were not wasted. Pastoral service surely aided his insight into the kind of preparation that was required before people could hear the Gospel with a sympathetic mind. As a preacher and a confidant, Newman never forgot what some evangelists seem never to learn: proof is not persuasion. What Newman modelled is that before the preacher can convince by argument, he must feel with sympathy; that before a preacher can name a hunger, he must sense his own poverty; that before he will move others to love, love must have moved him.[3] If we are to follow Newman's lead here, the contemporary evangelist must learn to feel deeply the hopes and fears of his audience. This is not easy. The hopes and fears of our contemporaries are often colored by a distinctively postmodern, post-Christian pathology. All men

2. Fulton Sheen, *Treasure in Clay: The Autobiography of Fulton Sheen* (New York, Image: 2008), 77–78.

3. Cf. *Idea*, 2.4, "University Preaching."

everywhere have sought happiness; a defining characteristic of our friends and neighbors is that we doubt we can win it.

Despite our lusty confidence in progress, despite our enormous success at conquering diseases and distances, we postmoderns are saddled with the fear of cosmic indifference. It is almost as though the more we try to defy nature, the less we feel at home in the world. Technological society has provoked many responses; among the most common, and the one Newman can help us interpret, is the sense of *dread.*

II

Certainly, preachers before Newman recognized the pedagogical value of fear. "The fear of the Lord is the beginning of wisdom," declares the Psalmist. Our "psychological age," when governments devote vast resources to promoting health and safety, when schools denounce bullying, when judging is forbidden, is also the age of ballooning debt, of bowling alone, of anxiety disorders, and of drug overdoses—now the leading cause of death in the United States for people under 50.[4] Despite affluence, sadness surrounds. The threat of final loss, of the possibility of the evil end of all things, that absurdity holds the last word, is a fear that disturbs our imagination more now than it did in the past.

We can miss this novelty. Enlightenment philosophers, and their present-day imitators in the media and in our schools, like to conjure in the public imagination a "middle ages" and other times saturated with faith, as obsessed with sex, hell, and the terrors of death. Indeed, since Marx, a common song has been that religion plays on men's fears, that the opiate of faith leads us to ignore the poor of this world. It may be that former ages thought more of death. This does

4. See the Center for Disease Control site: www.cdc.gov/drugoverdose/index.html, and see other sociological research in studies, such as Charles Murray's *Coming Apart: The State of White America* (New York: Crown Publishing, 2013), Robert Putnam's *Bowling Alone* (New York: Simon and Schuster, 2000), and *The Upswing: How Americans Came Together a Century Ago and How We Can Do It Again* (New York: Simon and Schuster, 2020).

not mean we think any better about life. Anyone familiar with the bright pageantry of the thirteenth and fourteenth centuries, or with the exuberant religious festivals of the fifteenth and sixteenth centuries, or with the literature from *Beowulf* to *The Canterbury Tales*, or with the music, drama, processions, and architecture that sprung out of the Baroque era, will find such a caricature of a joyless Christian culture unconvincing. Wherever the Church has thrived, culture has flowered. Recall that the greatest poem produced by the West, a poem structured around a tour of the houses of the dead, was named a divine *comedy.* This is no accident. Joy is an abiding feature of a culture that has learned to give thanks to its maker. During the Christian centuries and even recent decades, we knew that the story of the world ended aright. Now, we are not so sure.

In this regard, Newman, like Dostoevsky, was a herald of the nihilism to come. Newman was not alone among Victorians to feel deeply the "long, withdrawing roar" of the Sea of Faith, as Matthew Arnold named it.[5] As both an astute observer of his age and as one who attempted to shape its course, Newman was situated better than most to understand the disorientation of the nineteenth century. At a high point in his autobiography, for instance, he meditates upon the sadness and contradiction that afflicts the intelligence of modern men and women as we search for signs of order:

> To consider the world in its length and breadth, its various history, the many races of man, their starts, their fortunes, their mutual alienation, their conflicts; and then their ways, habits, governments, forms of worship; their enterprises, their aimless courses, their random achievements and acquirements, the impotent conclusion of long-standing facts, the tokens so faint and broken of a superintending design, the blind evolution of what turn out to be great powers or truths, the progress of things, as if from unreasoning elements, not towards final causes, the greatness and littleness of man, his far-reaching aims, his short duration, the curtain hung over his futurity, the disappointments of life, the defeat of good, the success of evil, physical pain, mental anguish, the prevalence and intensity of sin, the pervading idolatries, the corruptions, the

5. See his poem *Dover Beach.*

> dreary hopeless irreligion, that condition of the whole race, so fearfully yet exactly described in the Apostle's words, "having no hope and without God in the world,"—all this is a vision to dizzy and appal; and inflicts upon the mind the sense of a profound mystery, which is absolutely beyond human solution.[6]

It is the futility of sin that grips Newman. Even during his age of progress and science, of new machines, and of an expanding Empire, Newman saw and felt the tedium that always must accompany those who have no reason to hope for an everlasting reward.

III

Newman's literary achievement, sometimes overlooked by theologians, offers another view into our present disorientation. In his masterpiece, the *Dream of Gerontius*, Newman vividly expressed the creeping mood of late modernity. In his poem, Gerontius is a good man, a Christian even, who faces his last agony. The dream-poem depicts Gerontius's final moments on earth en route to purgatory, and relates his passion, wonder, indecision and, finally, conquest in the face of the devils' taunts. Gerontius's first sensations at the approach of death are of the fear of total loss. Newman's feeling for the fragility of human being, for the instability of the self, rivals the high poetry of Shakespeare and Calderón and anticipates the sensibility of later writers:

> As though my very being had given way,
> As though I was no more a substance now,
> And could fall back on nought to be my stay...
> And turn no whither, but must needs decay
> And drop from out the universal frame
> Into that shapeless, scopeless, blank abyss.
> That utter nothingness, of which I came...[7]

Hope totters along a slim edge. It is the dizzying prospect of annihilation that tempts Gerontius as he prepares to depart from the

6. *Apo* v, 241–42.
7. *VV* "Dream of Gerontius," 324.

world of sense. Newman, like T. S. Eliot, Samuel Beckett and Albert Camus and their generation of poets and playwrights, sets before our eye the dread that behind the cosmos stands only indifference, that at the dissolution of our elements we must "sink and sink/into the vast abyss" and that, as the demons chide, "Virtue and vice" are, in the end, "all the same."[8] Newman's proposals for cultural renewal retain their appeal, in part, because we still occupy the spiritual landscape he described. The nihilism of nineteenth century elites has become the ennui of twenty-first-century teens.

But the medicine is not all bitter. Though one side of Newman's "anthropological approach" takes our disorder seriously, the other turns to a more abiding passion: the heart's desire for love. Returning to *Callista*, Newman's one literary depiction of an individual's conversion to Christianity, it is the young heroine's longing for a stable affection, for happiness, rather than an argument from order, or miracles, or indeed even from conscience, that draws her to faith.[9] *Callista* depicts the turn of an attractive young Greek woman of the 3rd century AD from paganism, to nihilism, ultimately to Christianity. Set in an age remarkably like our own, when Gnosticism had displaced public religion, her conversion can be taken as an image of, or at least as an exemplar for, the experience of many contemporary converts.

Callista encounters Christianity as a child first through her nurse. She grew up a good pagan. She took delight in the gods, and felt joy in the beauty of nature. That early image of faith impressed upon her by her devout servant needed twenty years to come into focus. Along the way, somehow her passage from youth to womanhood stripped away her confidence. The old pagan myths now frustrated her reason and left her imagination cold. During the action of the novel, Callista is "postreligious." If Callista were alive today, you could recognize her as a clever university student, or perhaps one recently graduated with a degree in marketing, whose parents took her to church up till their divorce when she was twelve, a young woman who fell into college, then into and out of love during her

8. *VV* "Dream of Gerontius," 348.
9. An observation made well by Ker, *Newman on Vatican II*, 139.

junior and senior years, who has put off marriage until she can repay her loans, and now, in her late twenties, all of a sudden feels the weight of loneliness crashing upon her shoulders. Callista recollects:

> At home I used to lie awake at night longing for the morning, and crying out for the god of day. It was like choice wine to me, a cup of Chian, the first streaks of the Aurora, and I could hardly bear his bright coming, when he came to me like Semele, for rapture. How gloriously did he shoot over the hills! and then anon he rested awhile on the snowy summit of Olympus, as in some luminous shrine, gladdening the Phrygian plain. Fair, bright-haired god! thou art my worship, if Callista worships aught: but somehow I worship nothing now. I am weary.[10]

Callista's name in Greek means "beauty." Beauty is that aspect of being which is pleasurable to behold. Her very identity points us back to the soul's longing for that which never fails to move. If her character offers a compelling description of the cage of modern weariness, it also provides a living image of our route of escape. The longings of the heart and our appetite for beauty, Newman suggests, are the needles on our internal compass pointing us to our truest loves.

IV

Is the needle sound? In one of his notable Anglican sermons, "The Thought of God, the Stay of the Soul," Newman sketches what it would look like to be delivered from terminal sadness. This sermon develops a propaedeutic to Christian proclamation and well illustrates his "anthropological approach" to apologetics. If self-conscious weariness along with an awakened hunger for beauty constitutes the first stage of this propaedeutic—a condition reflected in Callista's name—reflection upon the positive conditions for happiness constitutes the second. The awakening of dread and the longing for happiness are not in and of themselves proofs for God; but

10. *Cal* 118.

they do offer trustworthy indications for what we are searching for, and for our need for love.

All men and women seek happiness. None of us can attain happiness apart from love. For Newman, our need for love imposes upon the mind a burden that none can ignore. His psychological analysis proceeds in this way. The human person, he argues, has faculties or powers that reach out toward given objects. The underlying structure of our psychology remains stable regardless of our metaphysical disagreements; needs remain, irrespective of our ideas about them. Newman observes, as did Aristotle his teacher, that flourishing arises when these faculties attain their proper object. We hunger, and we are satisfied by food; we thirst, and we find relief in water; we long for society, and we are gladdened in the company of friends. Beyond any of these goods, or traversing through them, though, fundamental appetites carry an additional quality: they seek *permanence*. Human desire reaches toward some coordinating, "ruling principle, object, or purpose." Our longing for affection, for companionship and love, stretches toward a love that may, indeed, be partially satisfied by the little loves of this life. Yet in addition to these little loves we need a great love; "the affections require," Newman insists, something more vast and more enduring "than anything created."[11]

For the man without God this deep satisfaction is elusive. He writes movingly of the absurdities of the heart that neglects its native hunger.

> What a truly wretched state is that coldness and dryness of soul, in which so many live and die, high and low, learned and unlearned. Many a great man, many a peasant, many a busy man, lives and dies with closed heart, with affections undeveloped, unexercised. You see the poor man, passing day after day, Sunday after Sunday, year after year, without a thought in his mind, to appearance almost like a stone. You see the educated man, full of thought, full of intelligence, full of action, but still with a stone heart, as cold and dead as regards his affections, as if he were the poor ignorant countryman. You see others, with warm affections, perhaps, for

11. *PPS* v. 314, 16.

> their families, with benevolent feelings towards their fellow-men, yet stopping there; centering their hearts on what is sure to fail them, as being perishable. Life passes, riches fly away, popularity is fickle, the senses decay, the world changes, friends die.

For the unredeemed man in the midst of his exile, the only constancy is flux, and the one certainty, doubt. Thus may the preacher be forewarned. Rocky soil won't give back life until it has been overturned by the furrow. The wise evangelist will learn how to break up the encrusted topsoil of our weary souls.

Newman's anthropological approach to apologetics puts psychology at the center. Sadness, confusion, anxiety, beauty, hope each become rungs upon the sacred ladder to our redemption, if only we would see them for what they can offer. This fragility of our nature serves as a prick to the mind and heart to keep us from rest, to urge us forward, to draw us deeper into the ocean of that love that cannot be measured and will not be drained. Peace does not lie upon the earth. But its roots have been planted here. God has visited us. The preacher continues:

> One alone is constant; One alone is true to us; One alone can be true; One alone can be all things to us; One alone can supply our needs; One alone can train us up to our full perfection; One alone can give a meaning to our complex and intricate nature; One alone can give us tune and harmony; One alone can form and possess us.[12]

For us who would lead others to that perfect love, Newman's evangelistic strategy emerges out of his broad pastoral experience, but also his deep reading of the classics and the Church fathers. Ancient philosophers like Plato and Aristotle launched their appeal for God from the premise of our desire for happiness; Church fathers like Augustine and Athanasius accepted this common starting point and then amplified our image of the goal. The unmoved mover moves within us, as says the Psalmist, "all your waves and billows have gone over me" (Ps 42:7, RSV). Happiness takes the face of Jesus Christ. The God-Man alone is he who "fulfills the one great need of

12. *PPS* v. 325–26.

human nature."[13] Awe, fear and hope come first; formal proofs, as needed, come later.

To close I draw a parallel. Bishop Robert Barron is arguably the premier Catholic evangelist in North America today. Following in the steps of Bishop Sheen he outlines a strategy similar to Cardinal Newman's in terms that are nevertheless his own. Like Newman, Barron champions what might be called a version of the anthropological approach. It likewise begins with our most evidently felt desires, then launches from that common ground into terrain less willingly explored. On the apologist's method, Barron writes:

> The best evangelical strategy is one that moves from the beautiful to the good and finally to the true. Especially within our cultural matrix, so dominated by relativism and the valorization of the right to create one's own system of meaning, commencing with either moral demand or the claim to truth will likely raise insuperable blocks in the person one wishes to evangelize. . . . The pattern is more or less as follows: first the beautiful (how wonderful!), then the good (I want to participate!) and finally the true (now I understand!).[14]

Our problem, Newman could have said, is not that we are antireligious. Our problem is that we have become subreligious. The work of the preacher among contemporary pagans is, before planting the seed, preparing the soil, and with that call in view we turn directly to the role of education.

13. Ker, *Newman on Vatican II*, 142.

14. See Robert Barron's reflections, "Evangelizing Through Beauty" (February 19, 2013), www.wordonfire.org/resources/article/evangelizing-through-beauty/.

9

Not Without Liberal Arts

"I have called the perfection or virtue of the intellect... enlargement of mind"[1]

I

One of the consuming pastoral questions of Newman's day concerned university education. Now that official persecution had ended, and the universities had again opened to Catholics, should parents send their children? How well could their faith survive in a non-Catholic setting? Though some restrictions had lifted, England remained Protestant, her universities were turning secular, and Catholic opinion was divided. Cardinal Manning, himself a convert from Anglicanism, like Newman a graduate of Oxford, and the leading English churchman of the late nineteenth century, led one camp. The spiritual and moral risks to Catholic youth, he argued, were too great. Catholic families should stay clear of Oxford and Cambridge. Catholics in Belgium, France, Ireland, and the United States were establishing their own universities. Catholics on the Island should do likewise. At the height of the controversy Manning wrote: "What we most fear is that Catholics may cast themselves willingly, or be drawn unconsciously, into the stream which is evidently carrying English society every year more and more decidedly and perceptibly towards worldliness and Rationalism."[2]

Newman's own approach was more pragmatic. The ideal, "the true normal condition of things" always would be to found a Cath-

1. *Idea*, 1.6.1, "Knowledge Viewed in Relation to Learning," 94.
2. Quoted in Walter Drumm in *The Old Palace: A History of the Oxford University Catholic Chaplaincy* (Dublin: Criterion Press, 1991), 23–45, and 33.

olic university. But "you must go by what is practicable," and so politics, finance, and opportunity all need to be weighed.[3] He himself had helped found the Catholic University of Ireland. At one point, he advocated for establishing a college at Oxford, though later he would encourage setting up a "mission," a pastoral presence embedded within or alongside the university's structure. "Mixed or unmixed education"—that is, education by Catholics alongside Protestants or agnostics—"is indeed a question of expedience," he wrote in 1863. Instead of a universal norm Newman suggested a pragmatic precept. In any case, a few years later the Vatican settled the issue. In 1867, at the prompting of the English Bishops, the Congregation of the Propaganda Fide issued the following declaration that would remain in force until just prior to Newman's death: "In the present case where there is an intrinsic and very serious danger to purity of morals as well as to faith . . . it is next to impossible to discover circumstances in which Catholics could without sin attend non-Catholic universities."[4]

The Vatican imposes no such prohibitions today. Yet the dangers have intensified and the questions remain. How well do our schools and colleges perpetuate the faith? Can we expect young people to remain faithful amidst faithless faculty? Where are new schools needed? Up until the 1960s, the Church relied upon the classical liberal arts tradition as a means to foster the faith and Catholic culture of our young. That confidence broke over subsequent decades as Christian institutions across North America severed themselves from their religious foundations.[5] In recent decades pockets of renewal have appeared. For those searching for ways to found or rebuild their institutions, Cardinal Newman provides sage counsel. Perhaps his most important insights lay in his articulation of the nature and purpose of the classical liberal arts. In the *Idea of a University* Newman argues persuasively that the Church looks to the

3. *Letter* to Wm. Monsell (January 12, 1865), 382.

4. Drumm, cited in *The Old Palace*, 28.

5. No one has told better that sad story than James Burtchaell, C.S.C., in his magisterial *The Dying of the Light: The Disengagement of Colleges and Universities from Their Christian Churches* (Grand Rapids, MI: William B. Eerdmans, 1998).

arts to help her promote three goods in particular: to counter scepticism, to cultivate a robust intellectual culture, and to reconcile faith and reason. The work of this chapter is to show how the success of the New Evangelization will greatly depend upon our willingness to recapture this same educational tradition.

II

To judge how best to recover classical education today, parents need to grasp what are the present conditions of our institutions. The conditions are bleak. Unlike nineteenth-century Oxford, public universities today insinuate an aggressively cynical scepticism that undermines the honest quest for truth in general and the possibility of accepting Christian faith in particular.[6] The Georgian brick and Gothic stone of many state and provincial university buildings still invite gratitude for the civilizational project they once advanced. Whatever other goods they serve, however, they now explicitly undermine Christianity and its cultural forms. If secularism produces a counterfeit culture, then we should not be surprised that it has offered its own educational alternative. Its fruits lie scattered everywhere across the lawns of the campus. At the origin of Western philosophy the Delphic oracle bid seekers "Know thyself." Today if you step onto campus and are male, white, or religious, or are simply searching to know the truth about beauty, love, or God, the ringing message is "Despise thyself." At least that's the *genius loci* haunting the halls of the social sciences and humanities.[7] In any case, without mentioning the rise of hook-up culture, the ravenous

6. As John C. Somerville puts it in his study *The Decline of the Secular University* (Oxford: Oxford University Press, 2006): in order to render itself useful once again to people interested in knowing the truth about justice and morality, at the least, the secular academy would need "to foster an intellectual culture that puts respect, appreciation, and humility on the same level as the one remaining academic virtue of suspicion" (at page 137).

7. On the empirical evidence for the entrenched biases against religious and political conservatives now rampant among American universities, see George Yancey's *Compromising Scholarship: Religious and Political Bias in American Higher Education* (Waco, TX: Baylor University Press, 2017); on the effects of the new

loneliness among students, or the lowering of intellectual standards, parents would do well to attend to a single indicator: the rise in deconversions. Take ten churchgoing high school seniors and, so those involved in campus ministry tell us, after attending university something like seven out of ten will drop out of church, and most won't return.[8] Parents who send their children to secular campuses, and even to many Catholic ones, simply cannot expect them to retain the faith of their fathers.[9]

Leaving aside other features of the academy, let's focus on the curriculum. When Newman lectured to members of the Catholic University of Dublin in 1854 (the text was later published as *The Idea of the University*), he could assume that his listeners were familiar with the classical model. This unbroken tradition, he reminds these and other listeners, was first established in Greece and Rome, taken up by the Fathers of the Church, extended by the Benedictines, then the Scholastics, then the Jesuits, and in general served as the foundation for secular and sacred learning in the West.[10] The seven liberal arts—grammar, logic, rhetoric (the trivium), along with geometry, arithmetic, astronomy, music (the quadrivium)—aim foremost to perfect the intellect.[11] While economics is a useful study, it is also, in this terminology, a study that is *servile*. One does not study supply and demand ratios for their own sake. One studies supply and demand to generate wealth. But on what to spend the money? That is a blank cheque that economists must leave others to fill in. By contrast, liberal arts are intrinsically worthwhile, and

---

approach to education on students, see Greg Lukianoff and Jonathan Haidt's *The Coddling of the American Mind: How Good Intentions and Bad Ideas Are Setting Up a Generation for Failure* (New York, NY: Penguin, 2018).

8. As, for instance, in this report by the national campus ministry organization *Campus Renewal*: www.campusrenewal.org/wp-content/uploads/2016/09/Campus-Renewal-Campus-Link-Grant-Proposal.pdf.

9. For background, see Burtchaell, *The Dying of the Light* and the Cardinal Newman Society's helpful study "Behaviors and Beliefs of Current and Recent Students at U.S. Catholic Colleges" in *Studies in Catholic Higher Education* (October 2008) available at www.newmansociety.org/wp-content/uploads/SICHE-October-2008-Wagner-11-03-081.pdf.

10. See also *OS* Sermon 12, "The Mission of St. Philip."

11. See *Idea*, "Christianity and Literature," and his *Sermon* 10, in *PPS*.

hence called "free" (liberal, *liber*). The arts are free from requiring some external justification. The intellect is simply worth the effort. The rewards the arts offer are of the sort that rust and moth do not destroy, or so Newman argued.

The arts perfect the intellect also in a secondary sense. They serve as a gateway to more difficult study. In the traditional curriculum, liberal arts were valued likewise because they trained the mind *how* to learn. Civilization is the result of reason's cultivation of nature. The liberal arts support culture because they make fruitful disciplines such as law and medicine, and make possible the study of literature and architecture and theology. "And thus a definite school of intellect was formed," Newman concludes, "founded on ideas and methods . . . of the highest and truest character."[12]

Newman could assume such a structure was familiar to his hearers. Today this message is novel. Even where memory remains, few defenders of the arts remain, either on the political left or on the right. The left's triumph during the curricular wars of the 1960s and 1970s dislodged the arts and humanities from their former position at the center of the undergraduate curriculum. As Newman observes, for centuries, the "great books" had served as the backbone of European, Western, and Christian education.[13] The cultural tsunami that swept away the classical works of literature and philosophy in the twentieth century was not replaced by another list of books. What replaced them was a series of vaguely defined commitments. In place of the Bible and Shakespeare, students were taught to revere "diversity" and "inclusion," with no corresponding effort to show how these terms might or might not fit within anything resembling a coherent account of justice. As for those on the political right, the liberal arts do not find uninterrupted support there either, although for differing reasons. Having lost the curriculum, political conservatives of recent decades turned attention to other prospects. Bewildered at the universities' scorn of religion, and at its embrace of Marxist economic and cultural theory, and encouraged by their own gains at elections, at least in the short

12. *Idea*, 2.1.4, "Christianity and Literature," 195.
13. Cf. ibid.

term, conservative parents from the 1960s to the 1990s generally contented themselves with letting the colleges and universities go their own paths. When they did send their sons and daughters to university it was not to departments of history or philosophy but to the schools of business and engineering.

III

This strategy was understandable but shortsighted. The revolution in the curriculum encouraged a series of unfortunate results. The first was a practical revision of the object of the institution. The temple of secular reason that remained the modern university of the early twentieth century was transformed by the end of the century into a center of careerism. In the twenty-first century, the institution has now morphed into an arena for social activism. The intense hatred within the universities and the media recently showered upon Professor Jordan Peterson, and the devotion of his supporters outside of university officialdom, gives some measure of the distance that now separates the divided cultures. To be sure, other interests keep their stake in the university. The needs of professions and the demands of industry still shape programs. But even here, the wall of separation that was supposed to guard the so-called STEM disciplines from interference from politics has proven scalable. Identity politics has triumphed. "Disinvitations" of speakers due to fear of violence by protesting students have become common.[14] "Diversity Deans" now regularly supervise hiring committees—and it is not intellectual diversity that they monitor. Hauntingly reminiscent of the transformation inflicted upon German academies during the 1930s, many English-speaking universities now require applicants for faculty positions to pass a "values" test.[15] For forty years new hires have been profiled according to race and sex, and now by one's

14. On this, see Lukianoff and Haidt, *The Coddling of the American Mind.*

15. Those inside and outside of the Academy do well to set side-by-side William Shire's account of higher education in *The Rise and Fall of the Third Reich* (New York: Simon and Schuster, 1960), 248–52 and F.A. Hayek's observations of academic life within Soviet Russia (see *The Road to Serfdom* [1944], 117) with the new demands

self-declared erotic orientations. Today if you will not sign off on gay marriage or trans-identities, even before the interview, you've often failed the entrance exam.

In the universities of Newman's time, theology and metaphysics were not so much proved false as ignored. He summarizes the movement then afoot in the nineteenth century that would gain strength throughout the twentieth century:

> Such is the tactic which a new school of philosophers adopt against Christian Theology. They have this characteristic, compared with former schools of infidelity, viz., the union of intense hatred with a large toleration of Theology. They are professedly civil to it, and run a race with it. They rely, not on any logical disproof of it, but on three considerations; first, on the effects of studies of whatever kind to indispose the mind towards other studies; next, on the special effect of modern sciences upon the imagination, prejudicial to revealed truth; and lastly, on the absorbing interest attached to those sciences from their marvellous results.[16]

Newman describes well the first phase of the secular university's decline. But with no coherent ruling center, other contenders arose, far less tolerant of theology than were Newman's adversaries. Over the twentieth century, in the professional disciplines, the state and the market dictated where funding would flow. In the humanities, Marx's and Nietzsche's critique of knowledge filled a moral void. In North America, it took until the 1970s for Theology departments to be transformed into Faculties of "Religious Studies"—that is, departments where scepticism toward religious truth claims is officially declared in favor of so-called scientific approaches to religion.[17] These days, it is not easy to find recognizably Catholic theology even within Catholic universities.

concerning race, indigenous knowledge, and sexual orientation made upon those hoping to enter a university career in modern North America. For fodder, see the job postings in the Humanities listed in the *Chronicle of Higher Education Times*.

16. *Idea*, 2.5.2, "Form of Infidelity of the Day," 303.

17. For background, see my essay "Catholic Education and the Culture of Life" in *Liberal Education and Canadian Political Culture*, ed. David Livingstone (Montreal: McGill-Queen's University Press, 2015).

Newman saw in outline where we were headed. Already in the 1850s, he had predicted that metaphysical scepticism would lead inexorably to the decline of the university. In one of his most penetrating lectures in *The Idea of a University*, he says that the "fundamental dogma" of the university's modern visionaries is "that nothing can be known for certain about the unseen world."[18] While rejecting the concept of truth did not require that universities embrace Critical Race Theory, it does make it difficult to rebut such theories. Once power replaces truth as the criterion for judgement, moral debates are set upon an entirely new footing. In any case, moral relativism is always an abstract proposal. No one acts upon the theory consistently. Our particular form of scepticism is yoked to a feckless moralism. Still living off of the accumulated capital of Christendom, and in the afterglow of Marxism, the modern academy joins an evangelical fervor for material advance with a passionate regard for victimhood.[19]

IV

What is to be done? Quite simply, liberal education needs to be rediscovered. The project of the New Evangelization will gain little traction unless we learn to harness the liberal arts again so as to counter the claims of such sceptics. Certainly, piety helps. Catholic universities generally still encourage service-learning opportunities. The corporal works of mercy are good. But unless professors have the courage to teach against easygoing relativism, the gains made on study trips overseas will be lost at home. Social justice serves neither justice nor society when it is twinned with the dogma that all truths are fluid. And that is the one dogma that can't be touched. As those Catholic institutions that welcomed faculty committed to Marxist and feminist cultural critiques have discovered, once tenure was gained, the guests soon had little tolerance for the host.

18. See *Idea*, 2.4.2, "A Form of Infidelity of the Day," 295.

19. For a timely meditation, see Douglas Murray's *The Madness of Crowds: Race, Gender, and Identity* (London: Bloomsbury, 2019).

Newman explains in positive terms how a classical curriculum can serve the cause of evangelization. In a stunning passage from the *Idea of a University* he names the need for what he calls "general religious knowledge." This is the level of knowledge of religion that a liberally educated Catholic, in his view, should strive for and hope to attain. His models for the modern student are drawn first from the apologists of the early Church.

> Nor will argument itself be out of place in the hands of laymen mixing with the world. As secular power, influence, or resources are never more suitably placed than when they are in the hands of Catholics, so secular knowledge and secular gifts are then best employed when they minister to Divine Revelation. Theologians inculcate the matter, and determine the details of that Revelation; they view it from within; philosophers view it from without, and this external view may be called the Philosophy of Religion, and the office of delineating it externally is most gracefully performed by laymen. In the first age laymen were most commonly the Apologists. Such were Justin, Tatian, Athenagoras, Aristides, Hermias, Minucius Felix, Arnobius, and Lactantius. In like manner in this age some of the most prominent defences of the Church are from laymen: as De Maistre, Chateaubriand, Nicolas, Montalembert, and others.

The liberal arts open doors. The liberal arts refine the appetites. Those who submit to her disciplines may feast at her banquets. Note too that it is not the subtleties of scholastic theology that Newman recommends but that the undergraduate master the "external" view of religion, that is, its philosophical preconditions and implications. As he continues, the whole history of the Church's apologetic tradition opens up to a student who has been classically trained. Liberal education grants to rich and poor a passport that allows the pilgrim to travel to beautiful lands that will bring him back to his own time and place refreshed and invigorated:

> They might surely study other works too, ancient and modern, written whether by ecclesiastics or laymen, which, although they do contain theology, nevertheless, in their structure and drift, are polemical. Such is Origen's great work against Celsus; and Tertullian's *Apology*; such some of the controversial treatises of Eusebius

> and Theodoret; or St. Augustine's *City of God*; or the tract of Vincentius Lirinensis. And I confess that I should not even object to portions of Bellarmine's *Controversies*, or to the work of Suarez on laws, or to Melchior Canus's treatises on the *Loci Theologici*. On these questions in detail, however—which are, I readily acknowledge, very delicate,—opinions may differ, even where the general principle is admitted; but, even if we confine ourselves strictly to the Philosophy, that is, the external contemplation, of Religion, we shall have a range of reading sufficiently wide, and as valuable in its practical application as it is liberal in its character. In it will be included what are commonly called the Evidences; and what is a subject of special interest at this day, the Notes of the Church.[20]

Does this curriculum seem too lofty? Perhaps. That doesn't make it less necessary. Among twenty-year-old Catholics, basic knowledge of Church history and doctrine has nearly vanished. If they knew the names of "David" or "Moses," it's likely they encountered these characters from a Disney film rather than from a catechism class. If they have gone to university, it's worse. Solid skills in logic have been substituted with what is euphemistically called "critical thinking"—a moral commitment not to commit. Theology encompasses more than apologetics. Sacred doctrine takes interest in more than the defense of the preambles of faith—of proving God's existence, of the possibility of revelation, of the immortality of the soul, of proofs from miracles, or generally what Newman above calls "evidences." However, neither can it afford to ignore these. In such a time, as much as answering questions, the apologist today is in the business of awakening needs that have been suppressed. We ought to enlist logic, rhetoric, history and literature to help awaken and stir what has been left to lie dormant in the basements of lonely TV rooms.

V

If the first fruit of a liberal education is a buttress against scepticism, the second is an immersion in an ennobling cultural inheritance. Can the New Evangelization get along without it? I suppose it might

20. *Idea*, 2.4.4, "Elementary Studies," 284–85.

try. But its results would remain stunted. The scholastic maxim "Grace perfects nature" applies to the cultural as much as the strictly intellectual domain. Culture is simply another name for a common life ordered to the highest goods. Catholicism offers salvation for individuals, yes, but that new life is always lived in communion with others. Man was born in a garden, but he is destined for a city, the New Jerusalem (cf. Rev 21). All the goods necessary to and resulting from our common life, therefore, must find their place, their rightly expressed order, within the Church's preaching of a "new" evangelization. The role of the family, the design of the city, the rhythm of the economy, indeed the treasury and expressed wisdom of music, poetry, dance, and all the arts and sciences that perfect human life are to find their place here in the Church's proclamation.

By way of illustration, consider briefly how the goods of history and literature can enrich the Church's proclamation. These two disciplines, central to the classical curriculum for centuries, share the common aim of initiating the young into a web of stories, moral lessons, and beautiful modes of speech. Through the study of the past, the young, it is held, are shielded against the tyranny of capricious fashions. History, frankly, makes the gossip over Facebook look boring. As Cicero said, *Historia est magistra vitae.*[21] History is the teacher of life, of the rise and fall of nations, of the impermanence of power, of the stability of the wisdom of the ages. Likewise, the classical literature of Greece and Rome, and the literature of Christian centuries, for Newman, provide the intellectual building blocks from which the Church has ever and shall always express herself. Jesus's birth was not an accident. No doubt, those committed to relativism and its political cousin multiculturalism will think this a taboo. How could God or the Church think one kind of literature in any way better than another? Well, that is the claim. Hellenism was no accident. Newman sees it as providential that God should prepare Greece and Rome as the cradle for Christian civilization ever after.

21. Cicero, *De Oratore*, 2.6.

> The world was to have certain intellectual teachers, and no others; Homer and Aristotle, with the poets and philosophers who circle round them, were to be the schoolmasters of all generations, and therefore the Latins, falling into the law on which the world's education was to be carried on, so added to the classical library as not to reverse or interfere with what had already been determined. And there was the more meaning in this arrangement, when it is considered that Greek was to be forgotten during many centuries, and the tradition of intellectual training to be conveyed through Latin; for thus the world was secured against the consequences of a loss which would have changed the character of its civilization.[22]

Could the list of Great Books vary from place to place? Yes, somewhat. I think a contemporary defender of these liberal arts could soften Newman's advice without abandoning his claim. No doubt a defense of the classical tradition could well selectively include within this circle of the world's treasury some non-Christian literature, where this is found to correspond to what is sometimes called the perennial philosophy. From the East, the *Analects* of Confucius comes to mind, or the *Epic of Gilgamesh* from Mesopotamia, or from Islam the philosophical adventure tale of *Ibn Tufayl*; not that any of these writings presents a higher wisdom than, say, the Book of Job or the tragedies of Sophocles, but familiarity with them gives access to a common reservoir of experience and insight across cultures. The Great Books of all nations bear witness, however obliquely, to an abiding order of justice. By reading them with care we set our own roots deep in the soil of human culture. If natural knowledge about happiness and the moral law is accessible to all peoples, how much more can we find within the culture of the Christian West! To ignore the accumulated wisdom of our classics, to remain ignorant of Plato, Augustine, Dante, Shakespeare, Austen, Dickens, would not be to liberate ourselves from the past; it would merely be to condemn ourselves to the tyranny of those fashionable but transient opinions of the present. Simply, we would be naive to think the new evangelization could do without the old books.

22. *Idea*, 2.1.4, "Christianity and Letters," 195.

VI

There is a final benefit which concerns faith and reason. This last fruit of liberal education expressed in the *Idea of a University* has to do less with imparting doctrines than with inculcating a particular habit of mind. Relating the relative claims of faith and reason, distinguishing their methods, illuminating their convergences, appreciating their mutual dependencies, is the work of a cultivated intellect. When a young person today rejects his faith, he typically has rejected a childish version of his faith. He hears that evolution disproves the Bible, and so the *Scientific American* becomes his new scripture. Educated opinion on CNN or the CBC convinces him that one should always think for oneself, and so he joins the masses at the next Earth Day rally.

There are genuine intellectual difficulties that anyone with faith must confront. But most defections are pitiably unnecessary. Even a few hours with Aristotle or Thomas or Galileo or Newman, for that matter, could dispel most of the common clouds of doubt that hang over university students' minds about the relative claims of science and religion. Here a distinction may help. Revealed Theology speaks of what God has told us about himself; physics, on the other hand, draws inferences from experience. The differences in their objects lead to differences in their methods. "The argumentative method of Theology," Newman concludes, is "deductive," whereas "Physics, at least on starting, is that of an empirical pursuit, or inductive."[23] As we saw in an earlier discussion, on account of this vast difference, we should no more believe that the conclusions of physics, which describe the phenomena of the natural world, could conflict with Revealed Theology, which describes chiefly the nature of the Creator, than we should expect the conclusions of the zoologist to wreak havoc on the work of the chemist.

The history of our language here as elsewhere is instructive. The term "university" shares its roots with "universe." Two Latin roots combine in both: "uni," *one*, and "versus," *turned*. As the universe is the place which the creator has *combined into a whole*, so the uni-

23. Ibid., 2.7.6, "Christianity and Physical Science," 331.

versity is that community where the *whole is explored* by human reason. Newman's opening line of *Idea of the University* is true to the etymology: the university he insists is the one "place of *teaching* universal *knowledge*."[24] The cosmos is vast but one; truths are many but may never contradict. This confidence in the *unity* of knowledge, the confidence which makes plausible an institution's claim to teach universal knowledge, is a theme central to Newman's *Idea of a University* and his work as a whole.

Contemporary apologists will benefit from exploring this theme. The unity of the university is grounded in the unity of God. Lose God, and you've lost the university. Multiversities, *our* universities, Newman would think a counterfeit because they are institutions which have kept the material of the medieval and renaissance schools while losing this inner form. It was the centuries-long conviction of this essential unity, secured and defended by the Catholic Church, that helped make possible in the West the centuries-long experience of the advance of science proceeding alongside the love of the Faith. This practical, communal, oft-repeated experience of the unity of knowledge encourages among those who share in this kind of formation a unity of intellectual vision.

Newman calls this enlarged capacity for vision what we have named an *integrative* habit of mind. It is a habit to which any intellectually inclined believer should aspire. An integrated habit of mind is a mind that has learned to think all the way to first principles, to make connections between disciplines, to recognize the difference that God makes to every domain of knowledge. Throughout these chapters we have in various ways described the benefits that an integrated habit confers. Here at last is Newman's voluminous account of this mental cultivation:

> That only is true enlargement of mind which is the power of viewing many things at once as one whole, of referring them severally to their true place in the universal system, of understanding their respective values, and determining their mutual dependence. Thus is that form of Universal Knowledge, of which I have on a former occasion spoken, set up in the individual intellect, and constitutes

24. Ibid., opening of the Preface, xxxvii.

> its perfection. Possessed of this real illumination, the mind never views any part of the extended subject-matter of Knowledge without recollecting that it is but a part, or without the associations which spring from this recollection. It makes every thing in some sort lead to every thing else; it would communicate the image of the whole to every separate portion, till that whole becomes in imagination like a spirit, every where pervading and penetrating its component parts, and giving them one definite meaning. Just as our bodily organs, when mentioned, recall their function in the body, as the word "creation" suggests the Creator, and "subjects" a sovereign, so, in the mind of the Philosopher, as we are abstractedly conceiving of him, the elements of the physical and moral world, sciences, arts, pursuits, ranks, offices, events, opinions, individualities, are all viewed as one, with correlative functions, and as gradually by successive combinations converging, one and all, to the true centre.

To have even "a portion of this illuminative reason," Newman continues, is the "highest state to which nature can aspire, in the way of intellect." This habit places the mind above the influences of chance and necessity, "above anxiety, suspense, unsettlement, and superstition, which is the lot of the many."[25] Coherence in the university is the institutional counterpart to the individual's enlargement of mind. Of the many gifts of the Church to the world, and Newman's wisdom for our time, this is surely one of the most precious. It was for Catholics once to found the universities; it will be for Catholics and those friends similarly in love with truth to reform them.

VII

With many universities now existing as publicly endowed centers of anticulture, what specific proposals might Newman recommend to advance the Church's reevangelization of the West? I conclude by offering three suggestions.

First, we need soberly to reckon what has been lost. What we lost was the Christian ethos and curriculum of our institutions. The loss

25. Ibid., 1.6.6, "Knowledge Viewed in its Relation to Learning," 104.

of the liberal arts marked the end of any theoretically coherent resistance to what we might call a technological mindset. In a technologically ordered academy, knowing loses its contemplative aspect. Learning is no longer viewed as the perfection of the mind but merely an extension of making, or preparation for a job. In our institutions what is much harder to find is a model of learning that is an act of receptive, loving attention to things *as they are*. Modern people habituated to such a mindset thus find it harder to contemplate, let alone perceive an order that they themselves do not impose. Knowledge for such people simply *is* power. Modern universities justify themselves insofar as they extend man's dominion. Nature presents herself as so much raw material ready to submit to will. And in the twenty-first century, that part of nature most subject to the whim of will is the human body, both by our willingness to kill it, and our hubris to redefine it. In the face of such a loss, a return to the mental disciplines imparted by the classical liberal arts would help instill the natural virtues that religion presupposes. Those Catholic universities that would help us rise from the catacombs would, at the least, restore a strong common core of classical texts mandated across the curriculum. They would agree to a list of Great Books. They would hire faculty who love them. Then they would have the pleasure of watching their students be transformed through them.

A second proposal: reformed academies need to restore a sense of the dignity and vocation of the human person. Classical literature should be enlisted toward this end. In another place Newman observed that "the heart is commonly reached not through the reason, but the imagination."[26] The education that Newman championed entails a baptism of both reason and the imagination. Reason has its role in defending the faith, but the deployment of symbol and myth at some level matters more. Along these lines, the twentieth-century Jesuit theologian John Courtney Murray, in an article written prior to the rise of the "nones," prior to state-sanctioned euthanasia, prior to the sexual revolution, prior to the Second Vatican Council, developed this insight about the present needs of the laity. At its origins, secularism finds its inspiration not so much in reason

26. *GA* part 1, ch. 4, sec. 3, 92.

as in myth, specifically "the myth of the self-sufficient man in the naturalist closed universe." Appeal to reason may demolish the justification for secularism; too often though it "leaves the myth untouched."[27] Where bare argument falls flat, signs and symbols can often elevate. In this way, we ought to mine the classical and Christian literature of our past and present for the needs of our future.

Newman's personal experience allowed him to speak credibly about the transformative power of literature. His own conversion was abetted by an encounter with goodness mediated by one of Italy's greatest writers. In the months leading up to his turn away from Anglicanism he read Manzoni's novel, *I promessi sposi* (*The Betrothed*). The vivid image of holiness portrayed by this classic of Italian literature made attractive to Newman what formerly seemed impossible. Two years later, at the same time that he began to contemplate founding his own monastic community, he confessed to a friend: "That Capuchin in the 'Promessi sposi' has stuck in my heart like a dart. I have never got over him."[28] We need argument, but we need images just as much. By returning us to works of classical and Christian literature, by immersing students in the whole circle of knowledge, by instilling true enlargement of mind, the scientist can learn to look through his microscope, the physicist his algorithm, the biologist his dish, without carrying the burden of having to believe that this one part of creation is the whole. It is not. Man has a physical aspect. But the moral, intellectual, and spiritual aspects of our nature are grasped by means other than scientific ones. Within Catholic colleges, it is good to introduce students to the *Ethics* of Aristotle; but the lessons contained in that classic will be better received if the soil of their hearts has first been prepared by other instruments, like Virgil's *Aeneid* or C. S. Lewis's *Chronicles of Narnia*. Newman's vision for liberal education is an antidote to that shriveled anthropology currently celebrated within the culture of death.

27. John Courtney Murray, S.J., "Towards a Theology for the Layman: The Pedagogical Problem," *Theological Studies* 5 (1944): 351, cited in Christopher and Deborah Ruddy, "Handing on the Faith to the 'New Athenians'" in *Handing on the Faith: The Church's Mission and Challenge*, ed. Robert P. Imbelli (New York: Crossroad Publishing, 2006), 132.

28. *LD* vii. 151; see discussion by Ker, *Newman at Vatican II*, 95–96.

Finally, a word on institutions. They cast the shadow of their founders. Our institutions need the inspiration of large souls. Benedict XVI summed up Newman's influence on schools and colleges by praising the unity between life and learning that he modeled:

> I would like to pay particular tribute to his vision for education, which has done so much to shape the *ethos* that is the driving force behind Catholic schools and colleges today. Firmly opposed to any reductive or utilitarian approach, he sought to achieve an educational environment in which intellectual training, moral discipline and religious commitment would come together.[29]

Certainly, let us rebuild our Catholic universities and colleges; let us build up our Newman centers and campus chaplaincies. But in all but a few places, the greatest prospects for success lay in other directions, in the schools.

With or without the university, parents still need to educate their young. We should continue to support university movements such as Focus, Catholic Christian Outreach, and the Newman Centers that dot North American campuses, but we should be honest about the degree of damage being inflicted in university classrooms. Some can become well formed at university—though by the time children are 18, for most, frankly, it's too late. From the point of view of Christian anthropology, the most important lessons in moral and mental formation occur relatively early. A fifteen-year-old who learns Latin, has read classical Roman and Christian history, has acted in Shakespeare's *Twelfth Night*, has memorized his catechism, has studied the basics of Aristotelian logic, can sing the *Regina Caeli* and prays the rosary with brothers and sisters and friends has had a taste for learning and culture that will not easily be spoiled by animal rights activists foraging along the shrubs and dark corners of campus. Given how difficult it is to reform a university, parents should focus first on reforming or founding classical elementary and high schools, or on homeschooling well. The more frequently faithfully Catholic high school graduates appear the more possible it becomes to reform or establish faithfully Catholic colleges. From

29. Benedict XVI, AEB.

antiquity up till his time, the tradition of the liberal arts knew tremendous stability both in its ends and in its pedagogical methods. The present task for budding academies and reforming colleges is not so much to discover new pedagogies. Our present work is to adapt and retool ones already tested in the laboratories of the ages. Newman would only commend the classical education movement now well underway within North America and bid it multiply.

Where to send our young? The maladies of the modern university diagnosed by Newman have only intensified. Not the liberal arts, but careerism and activism now animate the curriculum. Whereas Newman worried that Protestantism could weaken the faith of young Catholics, children today wrestle with second and third generation pathologies—scepticism, atheism, Marxism, feminism, transgenderism, transhumanism. Certainly, the Church can and will evangelize with or without higher academies. But our efforts will bear meager fruit without them. The Gospel demands not only an assent of the heart. It requires also the renewal of the mind, the transformation of the professions, and the conversion of culture. For that task, the classical liberal arts have been indispensable aids in past ages, and remain so in ours.

10

Newman's Second Spring

"and who can hope for miracles,
and such a miracle as this"[1]

The goal of this book has been to show how St. John Henry Newman's thought helps us better proclaim the Gospel to our post-Christian culture. Though fundamental problems remain constant, each era requires a fresh response, and a new outpouring of graces. In line with the reflections of recent popes, George Weigel has described the time Christians are now living through as the "Church of the New Evangelization."[2] For the next half century, and more, Catholicism in the West confronts the task not chiefly of maintaining institutions, however vital, nor of winning back Protestants, however salutary, nor of preaching to Moslems, however needful, but of insinuating the love and knowledge of Jesus Christ into peoples for whom the memory of faith has grown cold or been forgotten.

The West still commands vast markets and militaries. But our culture has long been living off of borrowed capital with no foreseeable schedule of repayment. Confidence in liberal democratic institutions wanes. Indeed, with the rise of postmodern, antiliberal approaches to politics based upon racial and sexual identities, "we have reached a point in history where the liberalism and modernity at the heart of Western civilization are at great risk on the level of

1. *OS* "Second Spring," 173.

2. See George Weigel's opening reflections in *The Next Pope: The Office of Peter and a Church in Mission* (San Francisco: Ignatius Press, 2020).

the ideas that sustain them."[3] Christians have not been immune from the pathologies of secularism. Within the Church, for decades already, national decline in birthrates has been mirrored by failing numbers of marriages and priestly vocations. Even as a majority of Catholics have since Vatican II claimed the privileges of "interpretive autonomy," and so become more comfortable within the milieu of secularism, as a Church our freedom to witness to the Theology of the Body, to mention one site of conflict, has constricted. Secularism now less frequently wears the mask of neutrality. Public atheism presumes a rejection of the transcendent as a public category. Under the new regime, scientism has not so much conquered religion as drained it of its cognitive significance. And with religion gone, reason seems to be going. At least it cannot help us solve the big questions that science never claimed to master. One consequence of this altered situation is that modern culture suffers from what Jürgen Habermas has called an "ethical abstinence."[4] Another consequence is that comfortable Catholicism within North America has concluded. Yet another is that the "nones" have become our new poor. The Church of the New Evangelization, if it is to survive in more than isolated pockets, needs to find ways of making attractive what the demographic preparing to assume leadership now finds alien and ugly. Answering the cry of these new poor identifies the specific work of the New Evangelization. For this task, Newman surely can give aid.

Why do we need Newman? We need him because he described well salient features of the fragmenting culture which the Church now confronts. A key theme in his works and one that runs throughout these pages is that modernity has produced a *counterfeit* culture. Secularism apes, parodies, and presupposes the images, vocabulary, and moral capital of Christian faith. Yet it does so without engendering any coherent organizing principle. One's head begins to ache. Walking through any big city in the modern West is like stepping amidst a symphony that has fired its conductor and then divided the sheets of the score among its strings and brass.

3. Helen Pluckrose and James Lindsay, *Cynical Theories*, 12.

4. Habermas, *The Dialectics of Secularization*, 43.

"Liberalism" was Newman's preferred term for what results. His most recent papal admirer described the effect of this cacophony as the "dictatorship of relativism." I write these words in 2023. Social conflicts arising from contradictory impulses continue to mount. To consider only a few that the presence of the Corona Virus has made plain: civil leaders told us they must close whole sectors of the economy because "every life matters," even as governments continued to pay to abort the young as an "essential service"; out of compassion for our well-being governments locked children behind glass walls as their grandparents died alone, while showing liberality to roaming mobs marching shoulder to shoulder often with violence *en masse*. Diversity was supposedly our strength, but woe to that Twitter user who dared to wonder aloud about the social costs of forcing masks upon all faces.

As I have tried to show, though important differences separate Victorian England from contemporary North America, there is more that unites ours to the age of Newman and Nietzsche than divides. Newman predicted how secularism would, in its attempt to parody Christianity, insinuate a long series of counterfeit goods. To name a few we have explored: in place of Christian freedom, a negative liberty; in place of transcendent art, the desecration of beauty; in place of Christian conscience, an atomized autonomy; in place of Catholic orthodoxy, a therapeutic celebration of the self; in place of the classical liberal arts, a utilitarian education fueled by political causes. Though a secular, arid, non-metaphysical reason no longer commands the esteem it once did, modernity's founding myths continue to bewitch. For the Church of the twenty-first century, Newman rises as an indispensable guide, simply because he saw far into our future.

Newman offers us still more. In addition to describing the contours of our present cave, he also marked a way out, to a mode of life more beautiful and more intellectually satisfying for the Church and for the world. To advance the Gospel anew under the inspiration of Newman, I close these reflections by identifying three concrete proposals for renewal.

The first task is to continue bringing our own house in order. Newman was ever a champion of theological pluralism and freedom of thought, rightly conceived.[5] But Christianity, for Newman, is not a system open to the revision of individuals. Doctrine develops, truth remains the same. Catholicism, he states frankly, "is one whole" and a system of thought that admits of "no compromise or modification."[6] Where Catholicism in the West failed over the last fifty years, chiefly and dramatically, was in enforcing let alone celebrating its own liturgical and devotional and catechetical norms. And, since the eruption of scandals in recent decades, those blemishes of the Bride of Christ exacerbated by a lack of internal discipline have only been laid bare for all to ponder.

Still, the 2020s are not the 1970s. We own fewer schools, claim fewer religious, and run fewer hospitals. But those remaining in the fold are gaining a deepening sense of mission. Renewal is God's work. The warmth of that Second Spring for which Newman longed is already being felt. We also must claim our role in welcoming it, as Newman did through his tireless efforts both in his writings and in his building up of institutions. Indeed, wherever believers have embraced a liturgically robust, artistically sumptuous, magisterially informed, evangelically confident, charismatically inspired orthodoxy, there have the cold winds of winter begun to give way to new life, often amidst small pockets of friends and families, sometimes serving together in nascent communities, never doubting that the Kingdom of God has burst into our midst. May the rivers run.

After the renewal of catechesis, the second task for the Church of the New Evangelization, I believe Newman would propose, is to undermine public atheism. Conversion, according to Newman, occurs most often because "converging and convincing" antecedent probabilities unite. Here is where culture matters for faith. Apart from the material and social aids of a Christian culture, assent to the truths of religion tends to remain notional, abstract and, in Newman's terms, *unreal*. Our task as evangelists, Newman insists, is to study the "testimony of psychological facts" as we find them in

5. See Newman's sustained meditation on true liberty of thought at *LDN*, chapter 6.

6. *Idea*, 1.8.2, "Knowledge Viewed in Relation to Religion," 138.

living human beings; we need to rest content with the mind "as God has made it," rather than insist that people should come to belief, say, solely by apologetics or merely by emotional appeals.[7] We need both. We need ideas to invigorate just as much as we need beautiful objects and souls to prepare good soil. And the soil needs thoughtful cultivation. Culture is that field where the "soft sacraments" of Christian joy are encountered by surprise. Reading in a park opposite from the statue of a missionary saint, a man looks up from his book to wonder why foreigners from a sophisticated world laid down their lives for strangers in a wild frontier; hearing the rustle of a nun's habit gliding across the classroom floor, a young girl at her desk feels an undreamt desire awaken and a vocation born; writing an essay on the *Rule of St. Benedict* in his "Introduction to Western Civ," a college freshman gains a new metric of nobility against which to judge the preoccupations of contemporaries lost in trivia; a church's Gothic arch, a grandmother's book of devotions, a Corpus Christi procession down Main Street, a neighbor's rosary hanging from her rearview mirror—Newman proposes that these and a hundred other seemingly random meetings converge often for us into a coherent act of loving assent. The Church cannot give up on culture. It is over such cultivated soil that the Spirit blows its warm breath of life.

There is one last theme I have tried to emphasize, a theme that brings together these others. Newman can teach us again how to draw faith and reason into a living, breathing, growing dialogue. Though a proliferation of spiritualities abound in multicultural North America, public atheism still vies as the chief competitor in the battle over who and what will shape the ethos of our common life. You need not renounce your faith to think like an unbeliever. All you need to do is never learn to "put on the mind of Christ." Scientism in our universities, reductionism in our anthropology, constructivism in our schools, addictions on the internet, and the blithe dismissal of faith in politics are all signs of a deformed habit of mind that results from a narrowing of one's view of knowledge to merely material causes. A new advance of cultural apologetics is

7. *GA* part 2, ch. 6, sec. 1, 164.

required, and indeed already underway. As with the study of St. Thomas Aquinas, those who would become disciples of St. John Henry Newman find themselves initiated into a distinctive style of Christian thinking. His doctrines are illuminating, his insights sharp, but it is his *integrating habit of mind* that we most need to recover. The Church must continue to recapture without fear the cultural territory—the classroom, the music hall, the courtroom—that over the past three generations was largely abandoned. Only those who can think in an integrated fashion about faith and reason will be equipped for such work. Atheism needs to be undressed; woke needs to be exposed; fidelity needs to be embraced; the coherence of faith needs to be celebrated. As violence increases, as vulgarity loses its shame, more and more will the connections between public godlessness and cultural decay become plain. Learning to think like Newman with an integrated habit of mind will teach us how to build up what has been broken. It will teach us how to think *as though God exists.*

Rebuilding the culture of the Church will at moments require retreat from the world. But Catholicism will never rest content to remain consigned to the margins of culture. Its own internal dynamism, its openness to reason and science, its capacity to negotiate cultural differences, its artistic grandeur, its missionary mandate—all these require that it seeks to penetrate all trades and professions, all arts and crafts, all laws and customs, all for the good of man, all for the glory of God. May the witness of Newman's life and his work, alongside his intercession, inspire us now during this opening era of the New Evangelization as we seek by our words and works to give an appealing witness to that kindly light.

Appendix:
Three Addresses

After completing this book, I wished to find some other way more directly to convey the beauty of Newman's original insights on secularism and evangelization. This short appendix is the result. For those who wish to deepen their study, the following includes a series of short speeches. Each address touches upon themes pertinent to the New Evangelization explored in the book. At the head of each speech I offer an explanation of its importance and of what you can expect to find, so the reader may pick and choose as suits his interest.

1. Newman's "Biglietto Speech" given at Rome, May 12, 1879 on the occasion of his investiture as Cardinal of the Roman Catholic Church.

2. Newman's sermon, "Infidelity of the Future," delivered October 2, 1873 at the opening of St. Bernard's Seminary.

3. Benedict XVI's "Address at the Vigil on the Eve of the Beatification of Newman," London, September 18, 2010.

I

"The Biglietto Speech"

Newman's Declaration Against Secularism at His Investiture Ceremony in Rome

Below we find Newman's own compressed statement of the work of his life. The occasion for this speech was the announcement on May 12, 1879, that Newman had been raised to the rank of Cardinal by Pope Leo XIII, in Rome. After receiving the news of this honor, in the presence of a small group of dignitaries, Newman offered this reply. Newman describes in a few hundred words what Charles Taylor's A Secular Age *(2007) attempts in a few hundred pages. Newman defines liberalism (his more typical term for "secularism") as it has unfolded during his life, expresses its effects, and declares why his ambition has been always to counter it, and by implication, why we should do the same. Those wishing to pursue themes raised in Chapters One and Three, on the rise of the "nones," will find Newman's observations here and in the next selection illuminating.*

And, if I ask your permission to continue my address to you, not in your musical language, but in my own dear mother tongue, it is because in the latter I can better express my feelings on this most gracious announcement which you have brought to me than if I attempted what is above me.

First of all then, I am led to speak of the wonder and profound gratitude which came upon me, and which is upon me still, at the condescension and love towards me of the Holy Father in singling me out for so immense an honor. It was a great surprise. Such an elevation had never come into my thoughts, and seemed to be out of keeping with all my antecedents. I had passed through many trials, but they were over; and now the end of all things had almost come to me, and I was at peace. And was it possible that after all I had lived through so many years for this?

Nor is it easy to see how I could have borne so great a shock, had not the Holy Father resolved on a second act of condescension towards me, which tempered it, and was to all who heard of it a touching evidence of his kindly and generous nature. He felt for me, and he told me the reasons why he raised me to this high position. Besides other words of encouragement, he said his act was a recognition of my zeal and good service for so many years in the Catholic cause; moreover, he judged it would give pleasure to English Catholics, and even to Protestant England, if I received some mark of his favor. After such gracious words from his Holiness, I should have been insensible and heartless if I had had scruples any longer.

This is what he had the kindness to say to me, and what could I want more? In a long course of years I have made many mistakes. I have nothing of that high perfection which belongs to the writings of Saints, *viz.*, that error cannot be found in them; but what I trust that I may claim all through what I have written, is this,—an honest intention, an absence of private ends, a temper of obedience, a willingness to be corrected, a dread of error, a desire to serve Holy Church, and, through Divine mercy, a fair measure of success. And, I rejoice to say, to one great mischief I have from the first opposed myself. For thirty, forty, fifty years I have resisted to the best of my powers the spirit of liberalism in religion. Never did Holy Church need champions against it more sorely than now, when, alas! it is an error overspreading, as a snare, the whole earth; and on this great occasion, when it is natural for one who is in my place to look out upon the world, and upon Holy Church as in it, and upon her future, it will not, I hope, be considered out of place, if I renew the protest against it which I have made so often.

Liberalism in religion is the doctrine that there is no positive truth in religion, but that one creed is as good as another, and this is the teaching which is gaining substance and force daily. It is inconsistent with any recognition of any religion, as *true*. It teaches that all are to be tolerated, for all are matters of opinion. Revealed religion is not a truth, but a sentiment and a taste; not an objective fact, not miraculous; and it is the right of each individual to make it say just what strikes his fancy. Devotion is not necessarily founded on faith. Men may go to Protestant Churches and to Catholic, may get good from both and belong to neither. They may fraternize together in spiritual thoughts and feelings, without having any views at all of doctrine in common, or seeing the need of them. Since, then, religion is so personal a peculiarity and so private a possession, we must of necessity ignore it in the intercourse of man with man. If a man puts on a new religion every morning, what is that to you? It is as impertinent to think about a man's religion as about his sources of income or his management of his family. Religion is in no sense the bond of society.

Hitherto the civil Power has been Christian. Even in countries separated from the Church, as in my own, the *dictum* was in force, when I was young, that: "Christianity was the law of the land." Now, everywhere that goodly framework of society, which is the creation of Christianity, is throwing off Christianity. The *dictum* to which I have referred, with a hundred others which followed upon it, is gone, or is going everywhere; and, by the end of the century, unless the Almighty interferes, it will be *forgotten*. Hitherto, it has been considered that religion alone, with its supernatural sanctions, was strong enough to secure submission of the masses of our population to law and order; now the Philosophers and Politicians are bent on satisfying this problem without the aid of Christianity. Instead of the Church's authority and teaching, they would substitute first of all a universal and a thoroughly secular education, calculated to bring home to every individual that to be orderly, industrious, and sober, is his personal interest. Then, for great working principles to take the place of religion, for the use of the masses thus carefully educated, it provides—the broad fundamental ethical truths, of justice, benevolence, veracity, and the like; proved experience; and those natural laws which exist and act spontaneously in society, and in social matters, whether physical or psychological; for instance, in government, trade, finance, sanitary experiments, and the intercourse of nations. As to Religion, it is a private luxury, which a man may have if he will; but which of course he must pay for, and which he must not obtrude upon others, or indulge in to their annoyance.

The general character of this great *apostasia* is one and the same everywhere; but in detail, and in character, it varies in different countries. For myself, I would rather speak of it in my own country, which I know. There, I think it threatens to have a formidable success; though it is not easy to see what will be its ultimate issue. At first sight it might be thought that Englishmen are too religious for a movement which, on the Continent, seems to be founded on infidelity; but the misfortune with us is, that, though it ends in infidelity as in other places, it does not necessarily arise out of infidelity. It must be recollected that the religious sects, which sprang up in England three centuries ago, and which are so powerful now, have ever been fiercely opposed to the Union of Church and State, and would advocate the un-Christianising of the monarchy and all that belongs to it, under the notion that such a catastrophe would make Christianity much more pure and much more powerful. Next the liberal principle is forced on us from the necessity of the case. Consider what follows from the very fact of these many sects. They constitute the religion, it is supposed, of half the population; and, recollect, our mode of government is popular. Every dozen men taken at random whom you meet in the streets has a share in political power—when you inquire into their forms of belief, perhaps they represent one or other of as many as seven religions; how can they possibly act together in municipal or in national matters, if each insists on the recognition of his own religious denomination? All action would be at a deadlock unless the subject of religion was ignored. We cannot help ourselves. And, thirdly, it must be borne in mind, that there is much in the liberalistic theory which is good and true; for example, not to say more, the precepts of justice, truthfulness, sobriety, self-command, benevolence, which, as I have already noted, are among its avowed principles, and the natural laws of society. It is not till we find that this array of principles is intended to supersede, to block out, religion, that we pronounce it to be evil. There never was a device of the Enemy so cleverly framed and with such promise of success. And already it has answered to the expectations which have been formed of it. It is sweeping into its own ranks great numbers of able, earnest, virtuous men, elderly men of approved antecedents, young men with a career before them.

Such is the state of things in England, and it is well that it should be realized by all of us; but it must not be supposed for a moment that I am afraid of it. I lament it deeply, because I foresee that it may be the ruin of many souls; but I have no fear at all that it really can do aught of serious harm to the Word of God, to Holy Church, to our Almighty King, the Lion of the tribe of Judah, Faithful and True, or to His Vicar on earth. Christianity has been too often in what seemed deadly peril, that we should fear for it any new trial now. So far is certain; on the other hand, what is uncertain, and in these great contests commonly is uncertain, and what is commonly a great surprise, when it is witnessed, is the particular mode by which, in the event, Providence rescues and saves His elect inheritance. Sometimes our enemy is turned into a friend; sometimes he is despoiled of that special virulence of evil which was so threatening; sometimes he falls to pieces of himself; sometimes he does just so much as is beneficial, and then is removed. Commonly the Church has nothing more to do than to go on in her own proper duties, in confidence and peace; to stand still and to see the salvation of God.

Mansueti hereditabunt terram,
Et delectabuntur in multitudine pacis.[1]

1. Psalm 36 (37): 11, "But the meek shall inherent the earth, and they will delight in the multitude of peace."

II

The Infidelity of the Future

Newman's Pointed Advice on
Christian Service in the Age of Intolerance

Pastoral planning has for too long proceeded as though we still inhabit a Christian culture. We do not. In this homily, delivered to seminarians at the opening of term, Newman banishes any such illusions. As in the past, Christianity must now fight for its survival and, even in North America, must strive earnestly to keep open a space in which the Gospel might be heard. This homily, delivered at the opening of St. Bernard's Seminary in 1873, describes some of the fundamental dynamics of secularization, already present in the nineteenth century. Though the text soberly anticipates a future of persecution, Newman knows that Providence allows nothing to go to waste; the persecution and suffering of Christians, likewise, will be used by God to bring about greater fidelity.

It is no common occasion of thankfulness to the Giver of all good, the Divine Head of the Church, that has led our Rt. Revd. Father, the Bishop of this Diocese, to call us this morning from our several homes to this place. It is with no common gladness, with no ordinary words of rejoicing and congratulations on their lips, that so many of his priests and of his devout laity have met him here today in consequence of his invitation. At length this Seminary is completed and in occupation, which has been for so long a course of years a vision before his mind, and the subject of his prayers and exertions. Years and years ago I have heard him say, that he never could be at rest, till he was enabled by God's mercy to accomplish this great work, and God has heard his persevering prayers and blessed his unwearied exertions. I might say with truth, that even before some of you, my dear Brethren, were born, or at least from the time that you were in your cradles, he, as the chief Pastor of this diocese, when as yet you knew him not, has been engaged in that great undertaking, of which you, by God's inscrutable grace, enjoy the benefits without your own labours.

It is indeed a great event in this diocese, a great event, I may say, in the history of English Catholics, that at length the injunctions of Ecumenical Councils, the tradition of the Church, the desire of the Sovereign Pontiff, are fulfilled among us, and the Bishop's Throne is erected not merely in a dwelling of brick or stone, in the midst of those in whom Christ is to be formed by his teaching, that they in turn may be the edification and light and strength of the generation which is to come after him.

This handing down of the truth from generation to generation is obviously the direct reason for the institution of seminaries for the education of the clergy. Christianity is one religious idea. Superhuman in its origin, it differs from all other religions. As man differs from quadruped, bird or reptile, so does Christianity differ from the superstitions, heresies, and philosophies which are around it. It has a theology and an ethical system of its own. This is its indestructible idea. How are we to secure and perpetuate in this world that gift from above? How are we to preserve to the Christian people this gift, so special, so divine, so easily hid or lost amid the imposing falsehoods with which the world abounds?

The divine provision is as follows. Each circle of Christians has its own priest, who is the representative of the divine idea to that circle in its theological and ethical aspects. He teaches his people, he catechizes their children, bringing them one and all into that form of doctrine, which is his own. But the Church is made up of *many* such circles. How are we to secure that they may *all* speak one and the same doctrine? and that the doctrine of the Apostles? Thus: by the rule that their respective priests should in their turn all be taught from one and the same centre, viz., their common Father, the Bishop of the diocese. They are educated in one school, that is, in one seminary; under the rule, by the voice and example of him who is the One Pastor of all those collections or circles of Christians, of whom they all in time to come are to be the teachers. Catholic doctrine, Catholic morals, Catholic worship and discipline, the Christian character, life, and conduct, all that is necessary for being a good priest, they learn one and all from this religious school, which is the appointed preparation for the ministerial offices. As youths are prepared for their secular calling by schools and teachers who teach what their calling requires, as there are classical schools, commercial schools, teachers for each profession, teachers of the several arts and sciences, so the sacred ministers of the Church are made true representatives of their Bishop when they are appointed to the charge of the Christian people, because they come from one centre of education and from the tutelage of one head.

Hence it is that St. Ignatius, the Martyr Bishop of Antioch, in the first century of the Church, speaking of the ecclesiastical hierarchy, comparing the union of the sacred orders with the Bishop, likens it to a harp which is in perfect tune. He says in his Epistle to the Ephesians, "It becomes you to concur in the mind of your Bishop, as indeed you do. For your estimable body of clergy, worthy of God, is in exact harmony with your Bishop, as the strings to the harp. Hence it is that in your unanimity and concordant charity Jesus Christ is sung. And one by one you take your parts in the choir, so as to sing with one voice through Jesus Christ to the Father that He may hear your petitions" (*ad Eph.* 4).

And if at all times this simple unity, this perfect understanding of the members with the Head, is necessary for the healthy action of the Church, especially is it necessary in these perilous times. I know that all times are perilous, and that in every time serious and anxious minds, alive to the honour of God and the needs of man, are apt to consider no times so perilous as their own. At all times the enemy of souls assaults with fury the Church which is their true Mother, and at least threatens and frightens when he fails in doing mischief. And all times have their special trials which others have not. And so far I will admit that there were certain specific dangers to Christians at certain other times, which do not exist in this time. Doubtless, but still admitting this, still I think that the trials which lie before us are such as would appall and make dizzy even such courageous hearts as St. Athanasius, St. Gregory I, or St. Gregory

VII. And they would confess that dark as the prospect of their own day was to them severally, ours has a darkness different in kind from any that has been before it.

The special peril of the time before us is the spread of that plague of infidelity, that the Apostles and our Lord Himself have predicted as the worst calamity of the last times of the Church. And at least a shadow, a typical image of the last times is coming over the world. I do not mean to presume to say that this is the last time, but that it has had the evil prerogative of being like that more terrible season, when it is said that the elect themselves will be in danger of falling away. This applies to all Christians in the world, but it concerns me at this moment, speaking to you, my dear Brethren, who are being educated for our own priesthood, to see how it is likely to be fulfilled in this country.

1. And first it is obvious that while the various religious bodies and sects which surround us according to God's permission have done untold harm to the cause of Catholic truth in their opposition to us, they have hitherto been of great service to us in shielding and sheltering us from the assaults of those who believed less than themselves or nothing at all. To take one instance, the approved miracles of the Saints are not more wonderful than the miracles of the Bible. Now the Church of England, the Wesleyans, the Dissenters, nay the Unitarians have defended the miracles of the Bible and thereby have given an indirect protection to the miracles of ecclesiastical history. Nay, some of their divines have maintained certain ecclesiastical miracles, as the appearance of the Cross to Constantine, the subterranean fire in Julian's attempt to build the Jewish Temple, etc. And so again the doctrines of the Holy Trinity, the Incarnation, Atonement, etc., though as strange to the reason as those Catholic doctrines which they reject, have been held by many of these bodies with more or less distinctness, and thereby we have been unassailed when we have taught them. But in these years before us it will be much if those outlying bodies are able to defend their own dogmatic professions. Most of them, nearly all of them, already give signs of the pestilence having appeared among them. And as time goes on, when there will be a crisis and a turning point, with each of

them, then it will be found that, instead of their position being in any sense a defence for us, it will be found in possession of the enemy. A remnant indeed may be faithful to their light, as the great Novatian body stood by the Catholics and suffered with them during the Arian troubles, but we shall in vain look for that safeguard from what may be called the orthodoxy of these Protestant communions, which we have hitherto profited by.

2. Again another disadvantage to us will arise from our very growth in numbers and influence in this country. The Catholic Religion, when it has a free course, always must be a power in a country. This is the mere consequence of its divine origin. While Catholics were few and oppressed by disabilities, they were suffered and were at peace. But now that those disabilities are taken off and Catholics are increasing in number, it is impossible that they should not come in collision with the opinions, the prejudices, the objects of a Protestant country, and that without fault on any side, except that the country is Protestant. Neither party will understand the other, and then the old grievances in history which this country has against Rome will be revived and operate to our disadvantage. It is true that this age is far more gentle, kind and generous than former ages, and Englishmen, in their ordinary state, are not cruel, but they may easily be led to believe that their generosity may be abused on our part, that they were unwise in liberating those who are in fact their mortal enemies. And this general feeling of fear of us may be such as, even with a show of reason, to turn against us even generous minds, so that from no fault of ours, but from the natural antagonism of a religion which cannot change with the new political states into which the whole world is gradually moulding itself, may place us in temporal difficulties, of which at present we have no anticipation.

And it cannot be denied that there is just now threatening the political world such a calamity. There are many influential men who think that things are not indeed ripe as yet for such a measure, but who look forward to the times, when whether the one or the other great political party in the State may make it their cry at the elections of a new Parliament, that they propose to lessen the influence of Catholics and circumscribe their privileges. And however this may be, two things, I think, are plain, that we shall become more and more objects of distrust to the nation at large, and that our Bishops and Priests will be associated in the minds of men with the political acts of foreign Catholics, and be regarded as members of one extended party in all countries, the enemies, as will be thought, of civil liberty and of national progress. In this way we may suffer disadvantages which have not weighed upon the Catholic Church since the age of Constantine.

3. I repeat, when Catholics are a small body in a country, they cannot easily become a mark for their enemies, but our prospect in this time before us is that we shall be so large that our concerns cannot be hid, and at the same time so unprotected that we cannot but suffer. No large body can be free from scandals from the misconduct of its members. In medieval times the Church had its courts in which it investigated and set right what was wrong, and that without the world knowing much about it. Now the state of things is the very reverse. With a whole population able to read, with cheap newspapers day by day conveying the news of every court, great and small to every home or even cottage, it is plain that we are at the mercy of even one unworthy member or false brother. It is true that the laws of libel are a great protection to us as to others. But the last few years have shown us what harm can be done us by the mere infirmities, not so much as the sins, of one or two weak minds. There is an immense store of curiosity directed upon us in this country, and in great measure an unkind, a malicious curiosity. If there ever was a time when one priest will be a spectacle to men and angels it is in the age now opening upon us.

4. Nor is this all. This general intelligence of every class of society, general but shallow, is the means of circulating all through the population all the misrepresentations which the enemies of the Church make of her faith and her teaching. Most falsehoods have some truth in them; at least those falsehoods which are perversions of the truth are the most successful. Again, when there is no falsehood, yet you know how strange truth may appear to minds unfamiliar with it. You know that the true religion must be full of mysteries—and

therefore to Catholicism, if to any profession, any body of men at all, applies the proverb that a fool may ask a hundred questions which a wise man cannot answer. It is scarcely possible so to answer inquiries or objections on a great number of points of our faith or practice, as to be intelligible or persuasive to them. And hence the popular antipathy to Catholicism seems, and will seem more and more, to be based upon reason, or common sense, so that first the charge will seem to all classes of men true that the Church stifles the reason of man, and next that, since it is impossible for educated men, such as her priests, to believe what is so opposite to reason, they must be hypocrites, professing what in their hearts they reject.

5. I have more to say on this subject. There are, after all, real difficulties in Revealed Religion. There are questions, in answer to which we can only say, "I do not know." There are arguments which cannot be met satisfactorily, from the nature of the case—because our minds, which can easily enough understand the objections, are not in their present state able to receive the true answer. Nay, human language perhaps has not words to express it in. Or again, perhaps the right answer is possible, and is set down in your books of theology, and you know it. But things look very different in the abstract and the concrete. You come into the world, and fall in with the living objector and inquirer, and your answer you find scattered to the winds. The objection comes to you now with the force of a living expositor of it, recommended by the earnestness and sincerity with which he holds it, with his simple conviction of its strength and accompanied by all the collateral or antecedent probabilities, which he heaps around it. You are not prepared for his objection being part of a system of thought, each part of which bears one way and supports the other parts. And he will appeal to any number of men, friends or others, who agree with him, and they each will appeal to him and all the rest to the effect that the Catholic view and arguments simply cannot be supported. Perhaps the little effect you produce by the arguments which you have been taught is such that you are quite disheartened and despond.

6. I am speaking of evils, which in their intensity and breadth are peculiar to these times. But I have not yet spoken of the root of all these falsehoods—the root as it ever has been, but hidden; but in this age exposed to view and unblushingly avowed—I mean, that spirit of infidelity itself which I began by referring to as the great evil of our times, though of course when I spoke of the practical force of the objections which we constantly hear and shall hear made to Christianity, I showed it is from this spirit that they gain their plausibility. The elementary proposition of this new philosophy which is now so threatening is this—that in all things we must go by reason, in nothing by faith, that things are known and are to be received so far as they can be proved. Its advocates say, all other knowledge has proof—why should religion be an exception? And the mode of proof is to advance from what we know to what we do not know, from sensible and tangible facts to sound conclusions. The world pursued the way of faith as regards physical nature, and what came of it? Why, that till three hundred years ago they believed, because it was the tradition, that the heavenly bodies were fixed in solid crystalline spheres and moved round the earth in the course of twenty-four hours. Why should not that method which has done so much in physics, avail also as regards that higher knowledge which the world has believed it had gained through revelation? There is no revelation from above. There is no exercise of faith. Seeing and proving is the only ground for believing. They go on to say, that since proof admits of degrees, a demonstration can hardly be had except in mathematics; we never can have simple knowledge; truths are only probably such. So that faith is a mistake in two ways. First, because it usurps the place of reason, and secondly because it implies an absolute assent to doctrines, and is dogmatic, which absolute assent is irrational. Accordingly you will find, certainly in the future, nay more, *even now, even now,* that the writers and thinkers of the day do not even believe there is a God. They do not believe either the *object*—a God personal, a Providence and a moral Governor; and secondly, what they *do* believe, viz., that there is some first cause or other, they do not believe with faith, absolutely, but as a probability.

You will say that their theories have been in the world and are no new thing. No. Individuals have put them forth, but they have not been current and popular ideas. Christianity has never yet had experience of a world simply irreligious. Perhaps China may be an exception. We do not know enough about it to speak, but consider what the Roman and Greek world was when Christianity appeared. It was full of superstition, not of infidelity. There was much unbelief in all as regards their mythology, and in every educated man, as to eternal punishment. But there was no casting off the idea of religion, and of unseen powers who governed the world. When they spoke of Fate, even here they considered that there was a great moral governance of the world carried on by fated laws. Their first principles were the same as ours. Even among the sceptics of Athens, St. Paul could appeal to the Unknown God. Even to the ignorant populace of Lystra he could speak of the living God who did them good from heaven. And so when the northern barbarians came down at a later age, they, amid all their superstitions, were believers in an unseen Providence and in the moral law. But we are now coming to a time when the world does not acknowledge our first principles. Of course I do not deny that, as in the revolted kingdom of Israel, there will be a remnant. The history of Elias is here a great consolation for us, for he was told from heaven that even in that time of idolatrous apostasy, there were seven thousand men who had not bowed their knees to Baal. Much more it may be expected now, when our Lord has come and the Gospel been preached to the whole world, that there will be a remnant who belong to the soul of the Church, though their eyes are not opened to acknowledge her who is their true Mother. But I speak first of the educated world, scientific, literary, political, professional, artistic—and next of the mass of town population, the two great classes on which the fortunes of England are turning: the thinking, speaking and acting England. My Brethren, you are coming into a world, if present appearances do not deceive, such as priests never came into before, that is, so far forth as you do go into it, so far as you go beyond your flocks, and so far as those flocks may be in great danger as under the influence of the prevailing epidemic.

That the discipline of a seminary is just that which is suited to meet the present state of things, it does not become me to attempt to suggest to you now—you, who have so much better, and so much more authoritative advisers—but I may be allowed perhaps to follow up what I have said to such conclusions as it seems to point to.

1. A seminary is the only true guarantee for the creation of the ecclesiastical spirit. And this is the primary and true weapon for meeting the age, not controversy. Of course every Catholic should have an intelligent appreciation of his religion, as St. Peter says, but still controversy is not the instrument by which the world is to be resisted and overcome. And this we shall see if we study that epistle, which comes with an authority of its own, as being put by the Holy Spirit into the mouth of him who was the chief of the Apostles. What he addresses to all Christians, is especially suitable for priests. Indeed he wrote it at a time when the duties of one and the other, as against the heathen world, were the same. In the first place he reminds them of what they really *were* as Christians, and surely we should take these words as belonging especially to us ecclesiastics. "You are a chosen generation, a kingly priesthood, a holy nation, a purchased people..." (1 Pet. 2:9).

In this ecclesiastical spirit, I will but mention a spirit of seriousness or recollection. We must gain the habit of feeling that we are in God's presence, that He sees what we are doing; and a liking that He does so, a love of knowing it, a delight in the reflection, "Thou, God, seest me." A priest who feels this deeply will never misbehave himself in mixed society. It will keep him from overfamiliarity with any of his people; it will keep him from too many words, from imprudent or unwise speaking; it will teach him to rule his thoughts. It will be a principle of detachment between him and even his own people; for he who is accustomed to lean on the Unseen God, will never be able really to attach himself to any of His creatures. And thus an elevation of mind will be created, which is the true weapon which he must use against the infidelity of the world. (Hence, what St. Peter says: 1:2, 12:15; 3:16.)

Now this I consider to be the true weapon by which the infidelity of the world is to be met.

2. And next, most important in the same warfare, and here too you

will see how it is connected with a Seminary, is a sound, accurate, complete knowledge of Catholic theology. This, though it is not controversial, is the best weapon (after a good life) *in* controversy. Any child, well instructed in the catechism, is, without intending it, a real missioner. And why? Because the world is full of doubtings and uncertainty, and of inconsistent doctrine—a clear consistent idea of revealed truth, on the contrary, cannot be found outside of the Catholic Church. Consistency, completeness, is a persuasive argument for a system being true. Certainly if it be inconsistent, it is not truth.

III

Benedict XVI on Newman's Legacy

The Pope Sees in Newman a Man Who Has Joined Sanctity and Intellectual Honesty to Moral Courage

Delivered on the Eve of Newman's 2010 Beatification in London, Pope Benedict XVI outlines the distinctive virtues that recommend Newman to the Church's universal admiration today, in this era that is dominated by cultural relativism and spiritual indifference. Newman, as Benedict views him, confronts us with a life that is prophetic as much in his teaching as in his personal witness. Newman reminds us, argues the pope, that "we were created to know truth"; only in finding that truth, which is Christ, will our "deepest human aspirations" be fulfilled.

My Brothers and Sisters in Christ: This is an evening of joy, of immense spiritual joy, for all of us. We are gathered here in prayerful vigil to prepare for tomorrow's Mass, during which a great son of this nation, Cardinal John Henry Newman, will be declared Blessed. How many people, in England and throughout the world, have longed for this moment! It is also a great joy for me, personally, to share this experience with you. As you know, Newman has long been an important influence in my own life and thought, as he has been for so many people beyond these isles. The drama of Newman's life invites us to examine our lives, to see them against the vast horizon of God's plan, and to grow in communion with the Church of every time and place: the Church of the apostles, the Church of the martyrs, the Church of the saints, the Church which Newman loved and to whose mission he devoted his entire life.

I thank Archbishop Peter Smith for his kind words of welcome in your name, and I am especially pleased to see the many young people who are present for this vigil. This evening, in the context of our common prayer, I would like to reflect with you about a few aspects of Newman's life which I consider very relevant to our lives as believers and to the life of the Church today.

Let me begin by recalling that Newman, by his own account, traced the course of his whole life back to a powerful experience of conversion which he had as a young man. It was an immediate experience of the truth of God's word, of the objective reality of Christian revelation as handed down in the Church. This experience, at once religious and intellectual, would inspire his vocation to be a minister of the Gospel, his discernment of the source of authoritative teaching in the Church of God, and his zeal for the renewal of ecclesial life in fidelity to the apostolic tradition. At the end of his life, Newman would describe his life's work as a struggle against the growing tendency to view religion as a purely private and subjective matter, a question of personal opinion. Here is the first lesson we can learn from his life: in our day, when an intellectual and moral relativism threatens to sap the very foundations of our society, Newman reminds us that, as men and women made in the image and likeness of God, we were created to know the truth, to find in that truth our ultimate freedom and the fulfilment of our deepest human aspirations. In a word, we are meant to know Christ, who is himself "the way, and the truth, and the life" (Jn 14:6).

Newman's life also teaches us that passion for the truth, intellectual honesty and genuine conversion are costly. The truth that sets us free cannot be kept to ourselves; it calls for testimony, it begs to be heard, and in the end its convincing power comes from itself and not from the human eloquence or arguments in which it may be couched. Not far from here, at Tyburn, great numbers of our brothers and sisters died for the faith; the witness of their fidelity to the end was ever more powerful than the inspired words that so many of them spoke before surrendering everything to the Lord. In our own time, the price to be paid for fidelity to the Gospel is no longer being hanged, drawn and quartered but it often involves being dismissed out of hand, ridiculed or parodied. And yet, the Church cannot withdraw from the task of proclaiming Christ and his Gospel as saving truth, the source of our ultimate happiness as individuals and as the foundation of a just and humane society.

Finally, Newman teaches us that if we have accepted the truth of Christ and committed our lives to him, there can be no separation between what we believe and the way we live our lives. Our every thought, word and action must be directed to the glory of God and the spread of his Kingdom. Newman understood this, and was the great champion of the prophetic office of the Christian laity. He saw clearly that we do not so much accept the truth in a purely intellectual act as embrace it in a spiritual dynamic that penetrates to the core of our being. Truth is passed on not merely by formal teaching, important as that is, but also by the witness of lives lived in integrity, fidelity and holiness; those who live in and by the truth instinctively recognize what is false and, precisely as false, inimical to the beauty and goodness which accompany the splendor of truth, *veritatis splendor.*

Tonight's first reading is the magnificent prayer in which Saint Paul asks that we be granted to know "the love of Christ which surpasses all understanding" (Eph 3:14–21). The Apostle prays that Christ may dwell in our hearts through faith (cf. Eph 3:17) and that we may come to "grasp, with all the saints, the breadth and the length, the height and the depth" of that love. Through faith we come to see God's word as a lamp for our steps and light for our path (cf. Ps 119:105). Newman, like the countless saints who preceded him along the path of Christian discipleship, taught that the "kindly light" of faith leads us to realize the truth about ourselves, our dignity as God's children, and the sublime destiny which awaits us in heaven. By letting the light of faith shine in our hearts, and by abiding in that light through our daily union with the Lord in prayer and participation in the lifegiving sacraments of the Church, we ourselves become light to those around us; we exercise our "prophetic office"; often, without even knowing it, we draw people one step closer to the Lord and his truth. Without the life of prayer, without the interior transformation which takes place through the grace of the sacraments, we cannot, in Newman's words, "radiate

Christ"; we become just another "clashing cymbal" (1 Cor 13:1) in a world filled with growing noise and confusion, filled with false paths leading only to heartbreak and illusion.

One of the Cardinal's best-loved meditations includes the words, "God has created me to do him some definite service. He has committed some work to me which he has not committed to another" (*Meditations on Christian Doctrine*). Here we see Newman's fine Christian realism, the point at which faith and life inevitably intersect. Faith is meant to bear fruit in the transformation of our world through the power of the Holy Spirit at work in the lives and activity of believers. No one who looks realistically at our world today could think that Christians can afford to go on with business as usual, ignoring the profound crisis of faith which has overtaken our society, or simply trusting that the patrimony of values handed down by the Christian centuries will continue to inspire and shape the future of our society. We know that in times of crisis and upheaval God has raised up great saints and prophets for the renewal of the Church and Christian society; we trust in his providence and we pray for his continued guidance. But each of us, in accordance with his or her state of life, is called to work for the advancement of God's Kingdom by imbuing temporal life with the values of the Gospel. Each of us has a mission, each of us is called to change the world, to work for a culture of life, a culture forged by love and respect for the dignity of each human person. As our Lord tells us in the Gospel we have just heard, our light must shine in the sight of all, so that, seeing our good works, they may give praise to our heavenly Father (cf. Mt 5:16).

Here I wish to say a special word to the many young people present. Dear young friends: only Jesus knows what "definite service" he has in mind for you. Be open to his voice resounding in the depths of your heart: even now his heart is speaking to your heart. Christ has need of families to remind the world of the dignity of human love and the beauty of family life. He needs men and women who devote their lives to the noble task of education, tending the young and forming them in the ways of the Gospel. He needs those who will consecrate their lives to the pursuit of perfect charity, following him in chastity, poverty and obedience, and serving him in the least of our brothers and sisters. He needs the powerful love of contemplative religious, who sustain the Church's witness and activity through their constant prayer. And he needs priests, good and holy priests, men who are willing to lay down their lives for their sheep. Ask our Lord what he has in mind for you! Ask him for the generosity to say "yes!" Do not be afraid to give yourself totally to Jesus. He will give you the grace you need to fulfil your vocation. Let me finish these few words by warmly inviting you to join me next year in Madrid for World Youth Day. It is always a wonderful occasion to grow in love for Christ and to be encouraged in a joyful life of faith along with thousands of other young people. I hope to see many of you there!

And now, dear friends, let us continue our vigil of prayer by preparing to encounter Christ, present among us in the Blessed Sacrament of the Altar. Together, in the silence of our common adoration, let us open our minds and hearts to his presence, his love, and the convincing power of his truth. In a special way, let us thank him for the enduring witness to that truth offered by Cardinal John Henry Newman. Trusting in his prayers, let us ask the Lord to illumine our path, and the path of all British society, with the kindly light of his truth, his love and his peace. Amen.

RYAN N. S. TOPPING is the author of ten books on education and culture, including *The Case for Catholic Education*, *The Elements of Rhetoric*, and *Rebuilding Catholic Culture*. He is the Director of the Benedict XVI Institute for the New Evangelization at Newman Theological College in Edmonton, Canada. He and his wife have ten children.

Printed in the USA
CPSIA information can be obtained
at www.ICGtesting.com
LVHW081243290124
770083LV00104B/389/J